Communications in Computer and Information Science 1202

Commenced Publication in 2007
Founding and Former Series Editors:
Simone Diniz Junqueira Barbosa, Phoebe Chen, Alfredo Cuzzocrea,
Xiaoyong Du, Orhun Kara, Ting Liu, Krishna M. Sivalingam,
Dominik Ślęzak, Takashi Washio, Xiaokang Yang, and Junsong Yuan

More information about this series at http://www.springer.com/series/7899

María J. Abásolo · Raoni Kulesza ·
Joaquín D. Pina Amargós (Eds.)

Applications and Usability of Interactive TV

8th Iberoamerican Conference, jAUTI 2019
Rio de Janeiro, Brazil, October 29 – November 1, 2019
Revised Selected Papers

 Springer

Editors
María J. Abásolo (iD)
National University of La Plata, Argentina
La Plata, Argentina

Raoni Kulesza (iD)
Federal University of Paraíba
João Pessoa, Brazil

Joaquín D. Pina Amargós (iD)
Technological University of Havana
"José Antonio Echeverría" (CUJAE)
Havana, Cuba

ISSN 1865-0929   ISSN 1865-0937 (electronic)
Communications in Computer and Information Science
ISBN 978-3-030-56573-2   ISBN 978-3-030-56574-9 (eBook)
https://doi.org/10.1007/978-3-030-56574-9

Preface

The 8th Iberoamerican Conference on Applications and Usability of Interactive TV (jAUTI 2019), was held during WebMedia 2019 XXV Brazilian Symposium on Multimedia and Web Systems, from October 29 to November 1 in Rio de Janeiro (Brazil). It was the 8th edition of a scientific event promoted by the RedAUTI Thematic Network on Applications and Usability of Interactive Digital Television, that currently consists of 32 research groups from universities in 13 Ibero-American countries (Argentina, Brazil, Colombia, Costa Rica, Cuba, Chile, Ecuador, España, Guatemala, Peru, Portugal, Uruguay, and Venezuela).

These proceedings contain a collection of 10 papers referring to the design, development, and user experiences of applications for Interactive Digital Television and related technologies applied to the improvement of people's lives from Ibero-America. They were selected from 35 papers accepted at the event after a peer-review process; they were later extended and underwent a second peer-review process.

November 2019

María J. Abásolo
Raoni Kulesza
Joaquín D. Pina Amargós

Organization

Program Chairs

María J. Abásolo — IIILIDI-CICPBA, National University of La Plata, Argentina
Raoni Kulesza — LAVID, Federal University of Paraíba, Brazil
Joaquín D. Pina Amargós — Technological University of Havana José Antonio Echeverría (CUJAE), Cuba

Program Committee

Pedro Almeida — University of Aveiro, Portugal
Sandra Baldassarri — University of Zaragoza, Spain
Valdecir Becker — Federal University of Paraíba, Brazil
Fernando Boronat — Polytechnic University of Valencia, Spain
José M. Buades Rubio — University of the Balearic Islands, Spain
Bernardo Cardoso — University of Aveiro, Portugal
Fernanda Chocron Miranda — Federal University of Pará, Brazil
César Collazos — University of Cauca, Colombia
Jorge Ferraz de Abreu — University of Aveiro, Portugal
Israel González Carrasco — University Carlos III, Spain
Manuel González Hidalgo — University of the Balearic Islands, Spain
Roberto Guerrero — National University of San Luis, Argentina
Anelise Jantsch — Federal University of Rio Grande do Sul, Brazil
Cristina Manresa Yee — University of the Balearic Islands, Spain
Oscar Mealha — University of Aveiro, Portugal
Francisco Montero — University of Castilla-La Mancha, Spain
Patrícia Oliveira — University of Aveiro, Portugal
Rita Oliveira — University of Aveiro, Portugal
Antoni Oliver — University of the Balearic Islands, Spain
Ana Pisco — University of Aveiro, Portugal
Alcina Prata — Higher School of Business and Administration ESCE, Portugal
Miguel A. Rodrigo Alonso — University of Córdoba, Spain
Rita Santos — University of Aveiro, Portugal
Telmo Silva — University of Aveiro, Portugal
Ana Velhinho — University of Aveiro, Portugal

Contents

Design and Development

Incorporation of Immediacy, Dynamics and Interactivity to Digital Terrestrial Television Services in Cuba Through TVC+

Joaquín D. Pina Amargós(✉)🆔, Raisa Socorro Llanes🆔,
David Paredes Miranda, Maykel Amador González,
and Dany L. Villarroel Ramos

Universidad Tecnológica de La Habana "José Antonio Echeverría" (CUJAE),
Havana, Cuba
{jpina,raisa,dparedes,maikel,dvillarroel}@ceis.cujae.edu.cu
http://cujae.edu.cu/comunidad/jpina

Abstract. Digital Terrestrial Television (DTT) is a modern emerging scenario that allows to transmit informative content using a medium of great penetration in most of the peoples of the world. However, currently DTT is mainly used to transmit entertainment multimedia content. On the other hand, useful content is scattered on the Internet, making it difficult for most people to appropriate it easy. This paper presents a software solution that demonstrate the possibilities of DTT in a real scenario. The solution called TVC+ collects useful information available on the Internet and integrates it with the DTT services. Some of its functionalities have already been deployed in Cuba, demonstrating their usefulness in some areas of UN Sustainable Development Goals 2030: Education, Health, Food and Heritage. The technologies used comply with FOSS philosophy, allowing it to be adapted to other existing technological scenarios. Developing countries find an unprecedented opportunity to transmit useful, significant, up-to-date information with a minimum cost reaching most households with only a television and a decoder box. The experiences gained may serve as a basis for other developing countries, although also developed, to promote the improvement of the people in this way.

Keywords: Microservices · Web standards · Interoperability

1 Introduction

In Cuba, there are 3.5 million TVs currently operating ([12], V.17, p. 409). According to [5], until the end of 2019 there was a coverage of more than 70%

Supported by Perez-Guerrero Trust Fund for South-South Cooperation (PGTF) United Nations Development Programme (UNDP) project INT/19/K08 and Ministry of Communications of Cuba.

regarding the population that today has access to the signal of digital terrestrial television (DTT) through the distribution of more than 2.2 million receivers that include the so-called setup-boxes and hybrid TVs (hereinafter, STB). The above figures demonstrate the crucial importance of TV to reach the majority of the population in a simple and cheap way [9]. DTT interactivity is one of the main functionalities incorporated into digital television through its value-added services [7]. The Fig. 1 shows a general scheme of DTT including interactivity as it exists worldwide. This scheme includes the communication capabilities of the STB with the Internet provider using the "Return Channel" and the communication of the same with accompanying display devices that in turn can be connected to the Internet [2].

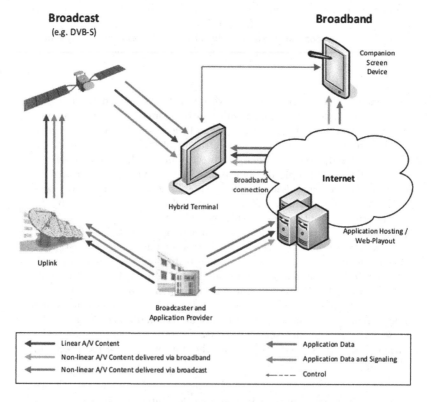

Fig. 1. General scheme of HbbTV (based on [2]). The arrows indicate the direction of the connection. The bottom box indicates the meaning of the colors of the different existing connections.

Despite the advances that exist worldwide in this regard, in Cuba there is only software and hardware that manages and displays content in plain, static text, of little relevance and usefulness to end users [14]. However, as indicated in [5], it is important to take advantage of the potential of value-added services, such as remote interactivity, to transmit useful information that can be received by the viewer. Currently the interactive services is presented to the viewer differently depending on the receiver installed. On the other hand, the specification that defines said service does not have the necessary flexibility to improve its functionality and visuality. Furthermore, the structure and content that is transmitted has little use for the population (see Fig. 2).

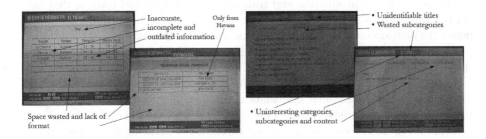

Fig. 2. Some pictures of screens showing the existing problems.

The authors of this work have proposed a solution that corrects the situation of updating information through the new technological platform TVC+. This software system allows content management manually but also automatically, as it is done internationally [3,4,10,11] from external RSS sources and Web services. Since September 2018, TVC+ is on trial and has continuously published more than 80,000 news from 13 external sources (Granma[1], Cubadebate[2], Instituto de Meteorología[3], La Papeleta[4], etc.) that are shown by all DTT receivers in the country. It is currently in the adjustment phase so that it is displayed in all types of STB following the Chinese specification [1] that defines its structure and formats. In this work, the main functionalities incorporated in TVC+ are exposed to incorporate the first elements of interactivity in Cuban DTT by using the data channel provided by the country's telecommunications company.

2   Proposed Solution

DTT allows the inclusion of data and software as an added value to the traditional audio and video stream. This data channel allows the viewer to delve into the audiovisual information that is transmitted and can even interact in a way that improves the traditional user experience as suggested internationally [13,15,16] (for example: consulting alerts on natural events such as tropical cyclones, synopsis and repertoire of the film, statistics of sports competition,

---

[1] http://www.granma.cu/feed/.
[2] http://www.cubadebate.cu/feed/.
[3] http://www.insmet.cu/asp/genesis.asp?TB0=RSSFEED/.
[4] http://www.lapapeleta.cult.cu/feeds/.

survey/examination to be answered, etc.). These functionalities are grouped in the so-called interactivity and depending on the connection requirement with telecommunication networks it is known as local and total interactivity. In Cuban television, for now, only local interactivity is possible due to the current limitations of the absence of the return channel, which makes bidirectional communication impossible. However, local interactivity is not yet sufficiently exploited due to inertia in the production and transmission of traditional content that has existed from the beginning. To solve the problem posed, the authors have proposed the development of a set of new functionalities that improve the updating and quality of the content that is transmitted by the current data channel. In this way, interactivity on Cuban TV is introduced in a phased manner, in a first stage locally and the conditions for full interactivity are prepared. The Fig. 3 shows how TVC+ obtains information from primary content sources using RSS and Web services standards. This content is packaged in the files that are transmitted so that they can be showed by the STBs. Among the implemented functions that improve the previous one, are:

1. allows to establish the order of the news,
2. incorporates a news approval flow,
3. maintains a trace log for future audits and reports,
4. automatically retrieves news from external RSS feeds and web services, making it easy to edit and improve the timeliness of its content,
5. enables access from any computer medium connected to the ICRT[5] intranet (national access and even from mobiles),
6. incorporates images by automatically adjusting their size and format so that they are displayed correctly in the STBs,
7. allows assigning permissions in a personalized way, even at specific sections and subsections level,
8. incorporates event and action management to achieve automatic content change dynamics and schedule management in an integrated way with the data service.

In the images generated by TVC+ it is proposed to include QR codes that encapsulate the interaction information. This code can be scanned by mobile phones that have a connection to the mobile data of the mobile phone provider (ETECSA[6]). In a first stage of the project, navigation and televoting QRs have been included (see Fig. 4). The idea allows expanding the potential of the data service transmitted by Cuban television without changing the current infrastructure. The scope of the proposal is very broad considering that TV is the medium that promotes informative content that reaches the population with the most penetration and duration. There is no history at the national level and the publication of some features proposed at the international level has not been found.

---

[5] Cuban Institute of Radio and Television (https://www.icrt.gob.cu/).
[6] Telecommunications Company of Cuba (http://www.etecsa.cu/).

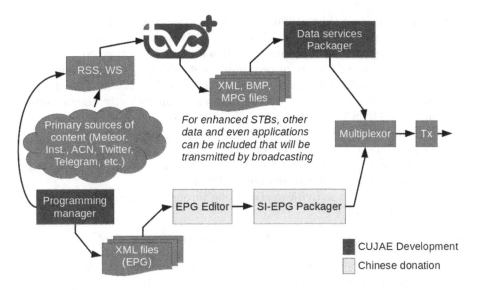

Fig. 3. General outline of the proposed solution in its initial deployment.

Fig. 4. Examples of using web browsing (left) and televoting by SMS (right).

The proposed functionalities are summarized below:

- automate the obtaining of content from primary sources identified as useful to the population,
- incorporate properties that indicate the period of publication of each news item,
- synchronize the news with the programs that are broadcast,
- incorporate event and action management to achieve automatic dynamics of content change:

Events: A certain time arriving, At the expiration of the publication time of a content (section, subsection or news), When certain content appears, By having or not having any news in a certain subsection, etc.

Actions: Change property of certain content (section, subsection or news) to a given value, Change format template, Publish certain content, etc.

- Incorporate content with a QR code that allows interactivity functionalities using the ETECSA data channel:
  - Televoting (SMS for voting or response selection),
  - Navigation (http URL to connect via browser) and
  - Payment of services by bank transfer (Account code to make payment by transfer through Transfermóvil APK[7])
- Management of the activities carried out through the data channel of the telephone provider.

Among the events and actions the following have been implemented:

- If a news item appears in a certain section or subsection (eg an alert) then certain subsections are hidden (eg sports and cultural).
- When the publication time of a news item expires, then the news item is moved to another subsection with another expiration time.
- If there is no news in a certain subsection then this subsection is hidden.
- If a subsection is hidden then certain subsections are displayed.
- If a certain program starts in a given period of time then a certain news is shown.

Novel technologies, free software and open standards were used on a layered architecture based on web services, allowing the extensibility and adaptability of the proposal (Apache, Node.js, AngularJS, MongoDB). The architecture of the TVC+ software allows the gradual incorporation of the interactivity elements, achieving their compatibility with current and future encoders. Currently, TVC+ provides the files specified in the Chinese documentation [1] as output, but the delivery of its structure and content has already begun to be implemented following other standards such as that specified in HbbTV [2]. The technological convergence currently proposed allows integration with other standards worldwide [8,17]. This aspect constitutes an important novelty that is presented in this work. The proposed solution allows the technological sovereignty of our country in this important area of knowledge with real future possibilities of exchange with other countries in the region.

3   Results and Discussion

The initial tests have been carried out in a controlled environment (see Fig. 5) using a modulator that transmits the signal generated on the PC from TVC+ and finally is displayed on the TV from an STB.

---

[7] Smart phones cuban software that allows online payment.

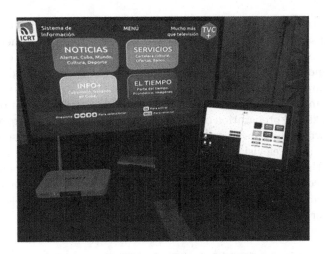

Fig. 5. Test scenario where the modulator is shown (in the center) that transmits the signal generated on the PC and is finally displayed on the TV from the STB.

After several months of stability in its operation, TVC+ has been deployed since September 27, 2018 and from that date it works continuously 24 h a day. Almost 200 new news items have been published every day and old ones are replaced to keep around 400 at any time. This software saves the country around 20 thousand USD considering that it is for a specific purpose. In addition, it reports a saving of resources equivalent to 5 thousand CUP each month taking into account that everything is done digitally, instantly and using the computing resources and network infrastructure currently installed in the ICRT (see Fig. 6).

Fig. 6. Deployment at Radio Reloj station on September 27, 2018.

All the institutions that provide useful information to the population can join the proposed solution (eg. governments at all levels to report on their management, Institute of Meteorology for part of the time and other useful ones such as agriculture and maritime, National Bus Company to inform the updated schedule of departures and arrivals, Pharmacy to inform the distribution of medicines, Bank to inform the exchange rates and schedules, Ministry of Education to guide extraclass tasks and preparation of entrance tests, Institute of Culture and Sports to report sports results such as the leaderboard of the National Baseball Series, Cuban Radio and Television Institute to transmit complementary information on programs that air and help the general culture and debate). They only have to publish their content using RSS standards and Web services following the service interface specifications defined in TVC+. Figure 7 shows the TVC+ dialog box where the user can edit the primary source from which the news is extracted.

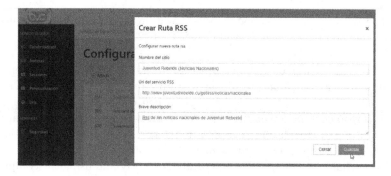

Fig. 7. News feed configuration dialog of TVC+.

For news sources, automatic news extraction reduces its out-of-date to just a few minutes. In the tests performed for the newspaper Juventud Rebelde[8], the oldest news was no longer than 24 h and the most recent was less than an hour. In addition, it should be noted that viewers enter to read the content of the interactive service to watch short news, which fit on a TV screen. In case the viewer is interested in deepening the news, TVC + indicates the primary source where he can find it. Figure 8 shows the entire process from the source URL to the preview of three news items published in the aforementioned newspaper.

The news is automatically obtained and shown to the viewer in real time with a few minutes of delay. This functionality is much more useful in case of early alerts to keep the population informed, even, without internet connection. Figure 9a) shows the news from the Cuban Meteorological Institute of a high-intensity hurricane. Figure 9b), c) and d) shows the preview of the three news items. It can be corroborated that the information is very useful to the population of the region and to the authorities for timely decision-making. Based on these results,

---

[8] http://www.juventudrebelde.cu/rss.

the authors of this work recommend including RSS channels in entities that can provide this type of information so that the processing is automatic and almost in real time.

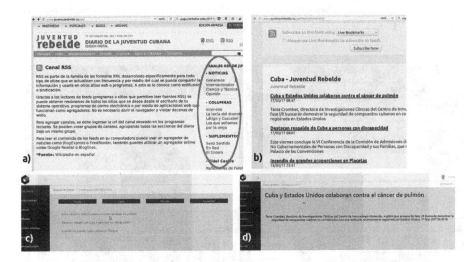

Fig. 8. Web page of the newspaper Juventud Rebelde highlighted in red circle (a) the RSS feeds; (b) view of the XML code returned by the RSS feed "Cuba"; (c) preview of news obtained automatically from the RSS feed; and (d) preview of the contents of a news.

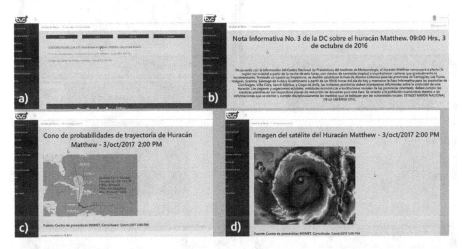

Fig. 9. Previewing news with the information note of the Civil Defense and the news with images indicating the trajectory and satellite photo of a hurricane.

The weather-related information is very valuable. TVC+ can report the weather behavior in real time, weather forecasts, early alerts, weather maps, etc. the information is extracted from the RSS channel of the Institute of Meteorology of Cuba[9] and the result is shown in the Fig. 10e) and f).

The Fig. 10 shows others examples that demonstrate the functionalities provided by TVC+.

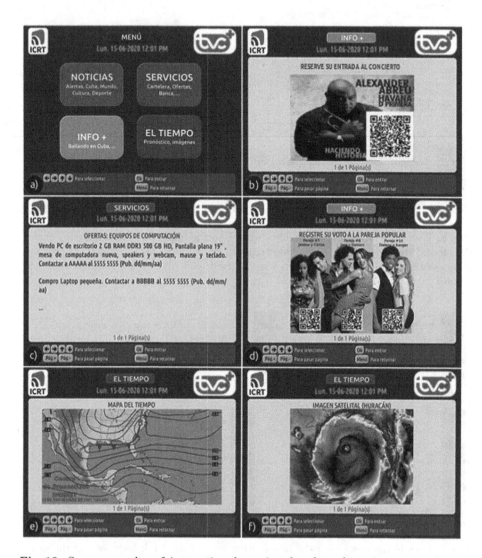

Fig. 10. Some examples of interactive dynamics that have been incorporated into TVC+.

---

[9] http://www.insmet.cu/asp/genesis.asp?TB0=RSSFEED.

Finally, the Fig. 11 shows the real-time preview of news related to the COVID-19 pandemic that is currently affecting the world. TVC+ extracts information from an RSS feed (Fig. 11a) and a Web service (Fig. 11b).

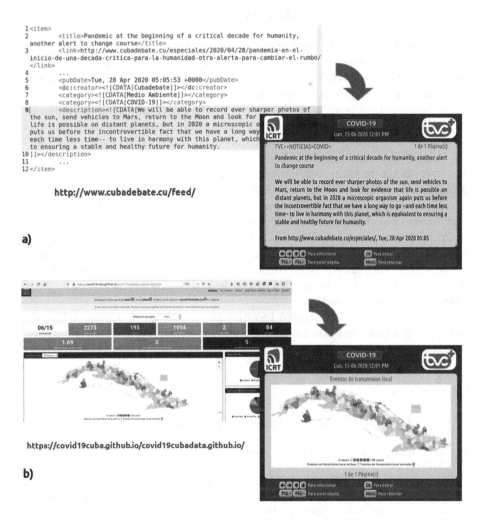

Fig. 11. Recent proposal for the use of TVC+ during the COVID-19 pandemic where the extraction and preview of a news is shown (a) from an RSS Feed and (b) from a Web service.

The results of this new solution shows tune with what was recently proposed by [6] to consider the innovation, information and social communication as the cornerstones in the management of the cuban Government, which has led to innovative solutions from science, the development of computer applications oriented to the confrontation of the pandemic and the exercise of social communication that has provided confidence and guidance to the population, while at the same time dignified with appreciable social recognition of the contribution of health staff and scientists.

4   Conclusions and Future Works

The proposed solution facilitates the dynamic management of the added value content of digital terrestrial television in Cuba and the gradual incorporation of the necessary elements of interactivity that allow its compatibility with current and future encoders. Some of these functionalities are already included in the TVC+ version that is currently deployed in the ICRT and have its endorsement. With the proposal, content can be generated that prepares the conditions for interactivity (complementary information on the program being transmitted, using a return channel via SMS or ETECSA's mobile data). The evolution towards interactivity is feasible by adding new functionalities while maintaining compatibility with current STBs. This solution allows the technological sovereignty of our country in this important area of knowledge with real future possibilities of exchange with other countries in the region.

From the proposed solution, it can be affirmed that the nascent Cuban software industry finds in this idea another door towards the computerization of Cuban society through the deployment of services that provide updated content of interest to homes and community places throughout the country, even without having an Internet connection.

As future work, it remains to test the functionalities in various STBs for their proper adjustment and to complete the implementation of the prototyped functionalities.

References

1. GY/T 201–2004. Specification for data broadcasting in digital television system (2004)
2. Association, H., et al.: Hbbtv 2.0.2 specification. SL: ETSI, 2018. TS (102 796, V1) (2018)
3. Barrero, A., Melendi, D., Pañeda, X.G., García, R., Pozueco, L.: Evaluation of text entry methods for interactive digital television applications with devices alternative to conventional remote controls. Int. J. Hum.-Comput. Interact. **32**(10), 765–776 (2016)
4. Calixto, G.M., Angeluci, A.C., Costa, L.C., de Deus Lopes, R., Zuffo, M.K.: Cloud computing applied to the development of global hybrid services and applications for interactive tv. In: 2013 IEEE International Symposium on Consumer Electronics (ISCE), pp. 283–284. IEEE (2013)
5. Cubadebate, R.: Televisión digital cubre más del 70 por ciento del territorio nacional. cubadebate (2019). http://www.cubadebate.cu/noticias/2019/11/06/television-digital-cubre-mas-del-70-por-ciento-del-territorio-nacional/. Accessed 6 November 2019

 6. Díaz-Canel-Bermúdez, M., Núñez-Jover, J.: Gestión gubernamental y ciencia cubana en el enfrentamiento a la COVID-19. Anales de la Academia de Ciencias de Cuba **10**(2), 881 (2020). http://www.revistaccuba.sld.cu/index.php/revacc/article/view/881
 7. ETSI: Digital video broadcasting (dvb); signaling and carriage of interactive applications and services in hybrid broadcast/broadband environments. TS (102 809 V1.3.1) (2017)
 8. Farias, B., Araújo, N., Fabrício, R., da Costa, J.B., de Lima Filho, E.B.: A methodology for convergence between ginga and HbbTV. In: 2019 IEEE International Conference on Consumer Electronics (ICCE), pp. 1–4 (2019)
 9. González-Neira, A., Quintas-Froufe, N.: Revisión del concepto de televisión social y sus audiencias. En: Quintas Froufe, N., y González Neira, A. (coord.), La participación de la audiencia en la televisión: de la audiencia activa a la social (13–26). Asociación para la Investigación de Medios de Comunicación, Madrid, España (2015)
10. Guzmán-Luna, J., Torres, I.D., Alvarez, J.F.: Propuesta de un generador de aplicaciones educativas basadas en televisión digital usando arquitectura de cómputo en la nube. Revista Colombiana de Tecnologías de Avanzada (RCTA) 2(24) (2017)
11. Martínez-Martínez, L.E., Martínez-Espinosa, L.: News reports on tv, twitter and the active audience. In: Applications and Usability of Interactive TV, pp. 121–133. Springer, Switzerland (2015)
12. ONEI: Informe final del Censo de población y viviendas de Cuba en el 2012. Oficina Nacional de Estadísticas e Información de Cuba (2014)
13. Paredes, D.: Alertas tempranas: Contexto de la televisión digital interactiva (tvdi). In: Anales de JAUTI 2013, II Jornadas Iberoamericanas de Difusión y Capacitación sobre Aplicaciones y Usabilidad de la Televisión Digital Interactiva, pp. 268–271 (2013)
14. Pina-Amargós, J., Álvarez-Goenaga, D., Villarroel-Ramos, D., Amador-González, M., Socorro-Llanes, R.: New functionalities of digital terrestrial television in cuba to contribute to the informatization of society. Revista Cubana de Ciencias Informáticas **12**, 158–172 (2018)
15. Ramirez, J., Marquina, D.A.P., Perez, N.: Usabilidad del diseño gráfico en los sistemas de alertas tempranas. In: VI International Conference on Interactive Digital TV IV Iberoamerican Conference on Applications and Usability of Interactive TV, p. 85 (2015)
16. Silva, T., Abreu, J., Antunes, M., Almeida, P., Silva, V., Santinha, G.: +TV4E: Interactive television as a support to push information about social services to the elderly. Procedia Comput. Sci. **100**, 580–585 (2016)
17. Sotelo, R., Joskowicz, J., Rondán, N.: An integrated broadcast-broadband system that merges ISDB-T with HbbTV 20. IEEE Trans. Broadcast. **64**(3), 709–720 (2018)

Toward Web Templates Support in Nested Context Language

Bruno Xavier Leitão$^{(\boxtimes)}$, Álan L. V. Guedes$^{(\boxtimes)}$, and Sérgio Colcher$^{(\boxtimes)}$

Pontifical Catholic University of Rio de Janeiro, Rio de Janeiro, Brazil
{brunoxl,alan}@telemidia.puc-rio.br, colcher@inf.puc-rio.br

Abstract. The Nested Context Language (NCL) are standards for multimedia application development for Digital TV. Some studies have indicated that NCL language is highly verbose. This factor increases the possibility of coding errors introduced by application developers. One way to reduce them is development based on reuse repeated elements in the code. On multimedia field literature, is common to use templates to active such goal. Templates describe a family of logically structured documents. Its adoption ends up in a reduction in the number of lines of code typed and thus make the final document less error-prone. On the web, templates are commonly employed in the development of Hypertext Markup Language (HTML) pages. In this scenario, developers use specific templates engines that can even run on the client-side, such as Jinja2 and Mustache. This work proposes provide an approach to support web template engines in the NCL applications development. More than that, it allows templates to be processed on the client-side, *i.e.* Ginga. By running on Ginga, developers can create applications with adaptable template-based content.

Keywords: NCL · HTML · Templates · Digital TV

1 Introduction

The Brazilian Digital TV System (SBTVD) Forum proposed the Ginga middleware for authoring multimedia interactive applications. Among others, it mandatory supports the execution of applications developed in the Nested Context Language (NCL) [3]. Today, both Ginga and NCL are ITU Recommendations for IPTV systems[1] and are used in TV systems in many countries of South America and Africa. NCL is based on XML[2] and consists of a domain-specific language for multimedia authoring. More precisely, it focuses on specifying multimedia applications with synchronized audiovisual media and key-based user interactions.

According to Soares Neto *et al.* [9], its syntax is verbose and error-prone. In this study, they concluded that programming in NCL becomes a hard job

---

[1] https://www.itu.int/rec/T-REC-H.761.
[2] https://www.w3.org/XML/.

© Springer Nature Switzerland AG 2020
M. J. Abásolo et al. (Eds.): jAUTI 2019, CCIS 1202, pp. 16–30, 2020.
https://doi.org/10.1007/978-3-030-56574-9_2

as applications' complexity increases. Based on this drawback, some works aim at supporting alternative formats (*i.e.* syntaxes) for NCL. One way to better support the development of NCL is code reuse based on templates.

Templates for NCL has been the object of study in several works. Among then, LuaTPL [1] and Luar [2], which evaluate Lua scripts inside NCL documents. Moreover, Terças *et. al.* [10] propose a markup language with a Lua-like syntax called sNCL. Finally, [6] and [8] present XML-based template languages for hypermedia documents, respectively, Xtemplate and TAL (Template Authoring Language). Despite these efforts, none of them obtained enough attention from NCL developers community. We take into account that, at the present moment, there is a shortage of NCL programmers.

Differently from the NCL development context, the usage of templates on the web has gained more and more attention from its developers' community. We can cite Jinja2 and Mustache as two widely used web-template languages. We believe that bringing web template languages to the development of applications in NCL strengthen this existing intersection by facilitating developers' work.

In the web scenario, it has become increasingly common to run template engines on the client-side. That is because, on the server-side, the server generates a new page for every interaction with a user. Each request has to travel all the way from the client to the server. Then, this page should be returned to this user. Such behavior can significantly increase the page loading time that may lead to latency issues.

Given this context, we define the following more specific question: *How can we improve NCL development template usage?* We argue that an option to improve NCL template usage is to leverage the use of these web template-based languages in the NCL development environment, exploring the natural intersection between NCL and web developers. Therefore, one of our objectives is *Evaluate web templates usage in NCL development*. Moreover, we also propose *Allow web template engines processing at Ginga i.e.* client-side.

The remaining of this document is organized as follows. Section 2 discusses related work and compare them according to some features relevant to our work. Section 3 presents the proposed approach to allow web template engines execution at both server- and client-side. Then, Sect. 4 presents a use case of web templates usage in the development of NCL applications. Finally, Sect. 5 discusses final remarks and the next steps.

2   Related Work

We organize related work into two groups according to their targeting language. The first group comprises those targeting HTML and the second those developed for NCL.

HTML Templates. Process HTML tags or special syntax elements in the HTML document to fill out information. We discuss in next the XSLT, Web components, Jinja2, Mustache, and React.

XSLT (eXtensible Stylesheet Language Transformations) [11] is a language for document transformations. Although it is a powerful language, creating changes requires non-trivial programming skills and deep knowledge on the target language semantics and structure. The transformations defined with XSLT are done in style sheets. One style sheet is specific to a single transformation, not being possible to reuse it in compositions containing elements different from the ones it was designed for. XSLT can operate over multiple input files in several distinct formats. The only requirement is the input file looks like XML.

Web components[3] allow developers to create new custom, reusable and encapsulated HTML tags. They consist on a set of JavaScript APIs (Application Programming Interface) to create such tags. These news tags act as components and widgets that will work across modern browsers. They accept styling and are only rendered after being processed by a JavaScript code. By themselves, they are not powerful due to logical structure limitations.

Jinja2[4] is one of the web's most used template engines. Its language is inspired by Django framework[5] template system, however, Jinja2 extends it with a more expressive language giving to template authors a more powerful set of tools. It may be employed for both HTML and XML formats. Jinja2 offers a complete tool set for handle templates *i.e.* provides not only the semantic and syntax necessary to a language but an engine as well. Such an engine is implemented in python, nonetheless, third-party implementations supporting other programming languages might be found. Among them, Lupa[6] written in Lua.

Mustache[7] is a logic-less template syntax. Such term comes out from the fact that it has no "if" statements, "else" clauses, or "for" loops. Instead, there are only tags. It works by expanding these tags in a template using values provided in a hash or object. Such tags are replaced with a value, some nothing, and others with a series of values. The language can be employed in HTML, config files, source code—anything. And, since Mustache supports various languages, it does not require a separate template engine on the server side. It is easier for non-programmers to manage once their logic is hidden behind tags. On the other hand, code became more difficult to read. Like Jinja2, it is implemented in many languages (e.g. Python, JavaScript, Lua). React[8] is a JavaScript library for building user interfaces on the web that runs on client- and server-side. It is based on the concept of reusable components. A component is a self-contained element (a function or class in JavaScript) that produces an output when rendered. They might include other components to build more complex applications. Despite not being a template language, React allows expressions through JSX[9] (JavaScript

---

[3] https://www.webcomponents.org/.
[4] https://github.com/pallets/jinja.
[5] https://www.djangoproject.com/.
[6] https://github.com/zhsso/lupa.
[7] https://mustache.github.io/.
[8] https://reactjs.org/.
[9] https://reactjs.org/docs/introducing-jsx.html.

XML), which embed XML code inside JavaScript. Similarly to Mustache, React code is also embedded in the HTML code.

When running on the web, Mustache and React works differently from Jinja2. The first two load their engines as a script and use the DOM (Document Object Model) API to edit the HTML document. The DOM enables JavaScript code to access HTML elements as objects in a tree-based data structure. On the other hand, Jinja2 loads the engine through importing statements.

NCL Templates. Handle new markup or special syntax elements in NCL. This group also comprises tools that process different languages to generate an NCL document. We discuss in next the TAL, XTemplate, LuaTPL, Luar, and Lua2NCL.

TAL [7,8] supports template specifications called incomplete hypermedia compositions. In TAL it is possible to define a set of documents that shares the same composition structure. However, it does not allow to assign its components information to the layout, nor does it provide any facility to create genre definitions of presentation characteristics. TAL owns template nesting, but its interfaces are not well-defined for this nesting, then properties can be violated.

XTemplate (3.0) [6] targets families of documents written in NCL 3.0. In XTemplate all users need some technical prerequisites such as XPath and XSLT [4], even if they only need to instantiate composition templates. XTemplate targets on easing the authoring performed by experts. On the contrary, TAL has as one of its goals the reduction for the need of experts. TAL avoids the use of external notations different from those of the target-language conceptual model and notations that are beyond the abstraction level (like XSLT processing instructions of XTemplate 3.0 does). XTemplate 3.0 was developed to a specific target hypermedia language. Unlike, TAL can be processed together with a padding document to generate applications in different target languages, depending only on the specific processor used.

LuaTPL implements its own special syntax and uses Lua language to process them. It is very limited in its capability and therefore, the development of sophisticated template becomes a very challenging task. Luar implements embedded Lua snippets in the NCL document. In Luar, used templates are indicated inside the padding and treated as a media object, instead of a document. Luar came up with the template component concept, that allows distinct templates combination to form more elaborated applications. It defines two distinct processors: one for template documents and another for applications.

Lua2NCL [5], a Lua framework that builds NCL tags through Lua tables, instead of XML, and then uses information on these tables to produce NCL documents. In Lua2NCL, some original NCL tags are removed while others become invisible to programmers.

To compare related works, we define four characterizes summarized in the Table 1. *Control structures Statements* indicates if the work supports control structures that change the template engine flow, such as loops and if-else statements; *Templates inheritance Statements*, means the capability of a template to inherit another. More precisely, one template acquires properties, states, and variables from its parents; *Component Statements*, indicates the support to components. Components are independent elements with a self-contained structure that may be assembled to build more complex applications; Main Reference Implementation column displays the target implementation language related to work; *Template Engine Languages* indicates the languages used to implement the engine.

Table 1. Related work features summary

Work	Control structures statements	Template inheritance statements	Components statements	Template engine languages
XSLT	for-each if-else	import	✗	Java, C, C++
webcomps.	JavaScript	✗	API	JavaScript
React	JavaScript	✗	React.Component	JavaScript
Jinja2	for-each if-else	extends	✗	Python, JavaScript, Lua...
Mustache	for-each	partials	✗	Ruby, JavaScript, Lua...
LuaTPL	Lua	✗	✗	Lua
Luar	Lua	✗	includeComponent	Lua
Lua2NCL	Lua	✗	✗	Lua
XTemplate	for-each	✗	✗	Java
TAL	for-each	extends	✗	Lua

3 NCL-Formats Tool

In Sect. 1, we asked *How can we improve NCL development template usage?* and we proposed to *Allow web template engines processing at Ginga* to approach it. To reach such goal, we build the NCL-formats[10] tool. It aims at assisting the development of NCL applications based on template languages, especially those targeting the web. Nonetheless, it is important to highlight that NCL-formats can handle a wide range of languages.

This approach takes advantage of the intersection between NCL and web development. With this perspective, we intend to bring web programmers and their knowledge to NCL development. Briefly, NCL-formats allows adding web templates language syntax to an NCL document. To the point of view of an application developer, it is just required to pass data (padding document) to a web-template engine.

The remaining of this chapter is organized to present NCL-formats. Section 3.1, defines which web-template language will be tested. Then, Sect. 3.2 addresses execution scenarios. At last, Sect. 3.3 comments about its implementation details.

---

[10] https://github.com/TeleMidia/ncl-formats.

3.1   Supported Web Template Languages

In the web context, it is common to benefit from repetition elements. One example is page headers that might be shown on several pages across one website. So, a web programmer may opt to use a template to build such headers. From this need, many template languages have been developed and innumerable options are available.

The following requirements were taken to define the languages adopted by this work: license should *not be proprietary*; have a *significant users base*; *support control structures*; *support template inheritance*; and being able to *run on DTV environment and on Ginga*.

Out of these four requirements, the most restrictive is the last one. In practical terms, it implies that the language should have an implementation in Lua. Such constraint eliminates a wide range of engines that targets languages direct related to the web development environment, such as JavaScript and PHP.

Based on these requirements, we chose to support Jinja2 and Mustache.

3.2   Templates Processing Scenarios

NCL-formats is a Lua script responsible for handle all the template processing. The choice for Lua is because it is Ginga's script language and its integration is straightforward. It can run on server- and client-side as well.

On serve-side, we focus on provide a standalone processing. Regarding running on the client-side, there are two options: *(a) extending Ginga Player* to support web template languages; and *(b) running template engine as a Lua Script*.

Standalone Template Processing. The standalone version enables developers to simulate their application on their workstation, for instance, making easier to create and test new template-based NCL applications. This scenario emphasizes that NCL-formats is self-contained and might be perfectly executed outside the Ginga environment.

The Listing 1.1 demonstrates NCL-formats execution through command line. The Lua script receives three arguments: the padding data; the template engine to be executed; and the template file itself. NCL-formats uses the template file name to generate the outputted NCL document.

Template Processing Extending Ginga Player. Extending the player implies in change Ginga implementation to process other formats. However, it presents itself with a great drawback: modifications on Ginga specification implies on new Forum and ABNT (*Brazilian Association of Technical Standards*) discussion to release a new standard. Moreover, it takes time to current STB (set-top box) and TV implement such features.

In this scenario, besides NCL documents, Ginga receives any template-based document *e.g.* Jinja2, Mustache. These documents are then handled by the NCL-formats tool that will processes information from padding documents to produce the final NCL document. After all, NCL player plays the generated NCL document.

```
1  lua ncl-formats.lua padding.json template_engine=jinja2
       template=slideShow_child.ncl.j2
```

Listing 1.1. Command line call to NCL-formats process Jinja2- and Mustache-based template for slideshow.

Ginga has been extended to support templates syntax. Ginga Parser checks the document type and if its a padding document it delivers the padding and the template to the corresponding engine. Then, this engine uses these two informations to generates the NCL document. After all, the NCL player collects the NCL document and plays it.

To aim that, a new option was added to Ginga's command line entry list. Such an option expects a template document and only validates if a padding document comes along with it. The Listing 1.2 illustrates its usage on the terminal.

```
1  ginga padding.json --template=slideShow_child.ncl.j2
```

Listing 1.2. PUC-Rio Ginga executing a Jinja template through command line.

Template Processing Embedded in an NCL Document. Motivated by the downsides of extending Ginga Player we opt for a solution that embeds template processing into an NCL document.

This approach is the main execution scenario for NCL-formats and it brings advantages compared to prepossessed templates: (1) does not imply any changes in Ginga as a standard; and (2) allows configuration at run-time. This last, results in great advantage as it gives more dynamism to generated templates.

In our solution the template engine becomes a script in Lua. By *running template engine as a Lua Script*, Ginga receives one single NCL document responsible for setting up the environment.

The Fig. 1 below examples how this process works. Ginga middleware receives the aforementioned NCL document with three pieces of information: template document; padding document; and template engine, as properties of a media object. This media object is the NCL-formats tool Lua script.

The Listing 1.3 next details this NCL document. The NCL player starts the Lua script with relevant information as a *property* of *NCL-formats.lua* script. The script uses the passed data to generate `final_documents.ncl`. On ending the script, the Ginga player starts to reproduce `final_documents.ncl`.

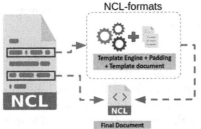

Fig. 1. Template processing through script languages

```
1   <ncl>
2   ...
3   <body>
4     <port id="template-handler" component="template-engine"/>
5     <media id="template-engine" src="ncl-formats.lua">
6        <property name="type" value="jinja2"/>
7        <property name="template" value="slideShow_child.ncl.j2"/>
8        <property name="padding" value="padding.json"/>
9     <media>
10    <media id="final-ncl" src="final_document.ncl"/>
11    <link id="link" xconnector="conBase#onEndStart">
12       <bind role="onEnd" component="template-engine"/>
13       <bind role="start" component="final-ncl"/>
14    </link>
15  </body>
16  </ncl>
```

Listing 1.3. Client-side template processing using NCL-formats.lua

3.3   Implementation Details

To work properly NCL-formats need to load some dependencies: JSON library, Mustache and Jinja2 implementation. The JSON library is necessary to dese-rialize JSON data from the padding document. In other words, this library is responsible for decoding JSON data and stores it in data type understandable by Lua language. It must be implemented in pure Lua, otherwise, Ginga is not able to execute it. The developed examples in Sect. 4 use JSON Encode/Decode in Pure LUA[11].

Mustache implements template inheritance through the concept of partials. Partials came from embedded Ruby (eRuby) and are used in this sense to refer to templates that cannot be rendered by themselves. Each partial must corre-spond to a file. Its Lua implementation is called Lustache[12]. It only handles templates as strings. So, in the scenario of a large Ginga application with n partials implemented, NCL-formats should read these partials (files) one by one

---

[11] http://regex.info/blog/lua/json.
[12] https://github.com/Olivine-Labs/lustache.

saving them as strings. Only after this data type conversion, the engine becomes able to process the template.

Jinja2's implementation is Lupa. It allows templates to be loaded from the same folder besides strings. When loading from folders, the developer only passes one template. The engine deals with any other required template, as long as they are in the same directory from the given one. Jinja2 implements variables that give more control to the programmers, such as `{{loop.index}}` and `{{loop.length}}` that counts the number of loop iterations starting from one and gets back the size of an iterable, respectively. On Jinja2 it is also possible to set up variables.

4   Study Case

This section presents an evaluation of web-templates languages behavior to built NCL applications. For that, it is necessary to discuss the evaluation procedure, first.

The **number of lines of code** is adopted as a metric for measuring the amount of work spent to produce an NCL application based on the chosen language. To determine an application's total gain, the Eq. (1) is used, where *TemplateLanguage* indicates the proper web-template language and *total percentage score* gives the percentage gain.

$$Score = \left[1 - \frac{number\ of\ [TemplateLanguage]\ lines\ of\ code}{number\ of\ NCL\ lines\ of\ code}\right] \times 100\% \quad (1)$$

Measuring the number of lines of code is not fair enough. It is unlikely different developers would code the same way. One programmer could type his code in just a few lines, while another may develop the same logic, using a larger number of lines, though. So, taking that into account we also use the **number of instructions** as a metric. Equation (2) demonstrates it.

$$Score = \left[1 - \frac{number\ of\ [TemplateLanguage]\ instructions}{number\ of\ NCL\ instructions}\right] \times 100\% \quad (2)$$

Due to NCL syntax, developers should type many instructions to specify their program and sometimes they do copying and pasting as a manner to reduce typing and gain time. The amount of code typed or the copy and paste process leads to errors in the final code that may pass unseen for developers until the application is tested.

The slideshow application illustrates this situation very well once it consists on several similar NCL links repeated over the code. It is a kind of presentation that changes the content displayed from time to time or after an action being triggered, *e.g.* user press a button to go back and forth. The final NCL document outputted by the two languages (Jinja2 and Mustache) are the same.

The slideshow example was build taking advantage of Jinja2's template inheritance capacity. In the example, there are two template documents: one called slideShow_base.ncl.j2 and the other slideShow_child.ncl.j2. Listing 1.4 and Listing 1.5 show them, respectively. SlideShow_base.ncl.j2 works as a base template in template hierarchy and is a NCL-based code with block tags in Jinja2 syntax. A {% block %} element indicates code replacement. So, in this case, a {% block medias %} indicates another template will handle this block. Same for the block {% block links %} links.

Logical structure is held in slideShow_child.ncl.j2 which is a child template. It takes over blocks on its parent. Inheritance is made through {% extend %} statement on slideShow_base.ncl.j2 file. Medias "block" generates the name of each media, gather its path and set them to id and src NCL attributes, respectively. Links block, builds a link passing media objects id formed in media block.

```
1   <ncl id="slideShow">
2     <head>
3     <regionBase>
4       <region id="main" width="100%" height="100%" zIndex="1"/>
5     </regionBase>
6     <descriptorBase>
7       <descriptor id="ImageDes" region="main" explicitDur="5s"/>
8     </descriptorBase>
9     </head>
10    <body>
11    <port id="startSlideShow" component="image1"/>
12    {% block medias %}{% endblock medias %}
13    {% block links %}{% endblock links %}
14    </body>
15  </ncl>
```

Listing 1.4. slideShow_base.ncl.j2

As well as in the Jinja2 example, the slideshow made in Mustache also was developed exploring inheritance. The slideshow proposed example, was developed based on the following files: slideShow.ncl.mustache, deals with NCL code that has not become a template; medias.mustache, builds the media NCL elements; links.mustache creates each link.

The code on slideShow.ncl.mustache document declares NCL code and calls the partials. Each partial corresponds to one file. Listing 1.6 displays its code. The head elements were removed for being the same as the Jinja2 instance.

```
1   {% extends "slideShow_base.ncl.j2" %}
2   {% block medias %}
3     {% for i in files_list[0].contents %}
4     <media id="{{`image' ~ loop.index}}" src="{{ `media/' ~ i.name
          }}" descriptor="ImageDes"/>
5     {% endfor %}
6   {% endblock medias %}
7   {% block links %}
8     {% for i in range(files_list[0].contents | length-1)guages.
          Therefor, we are also planning to extend it. It can
          support the current %}
9     <link id="{{`lMoveForward' ~ loop.index}}" xconnector="conBase
          #onEndStart">
10      <bind role="onEnd" component="{{`image' ~ loop.index}}"/>
11      <bind role="start" component="{{`image' ~ (loop.index+1)
          }}"/>
12    </link>
13    {% endfor %}
14  {%endblock links %}
```

Listing 1.5: slideShow_child.ncl.j2

Listing 1.7 and 1.8 next exhibits, respectively, the `medias.mustache` and the `link.mustache` file.

```
1   <ncl id="slideShow">
2     <head>
3       ...
4     </head>
5     <body>
6     <port id="startSlideShow" component="image1"/>
7       {{>medias}}
8       {{>links}}
9     </body>
10  </ncl>
```

Listing 1.6. slideShow.ncl.mustache

In the slideshow instance above, it is seen a reduction in the number of programmed lines.

On Jinja2, 36 lines of code overall were written, 16 of them related to template syntax while the others are in NCL. This code, when the final NCL document is generated, expands to a total of 119 lines of code. That represents a *score* of **69,75%**. From the overall number of lines, one is for inheritance and two are to delimiter the beginning and ending of which block tag. Considering, inheritance is not strictly necessary and everything could have been done in only one file we have 20 lines of code. That enlarges the score to **77,31%**. Now, considering the number of instructions the score becomes **76,92%**. And without a hierarchy structure, it raises to **82,42%**.

```
1  {{#contents}}
2    {{#index}}
3      <media id='image{{index}}' src='media/{{name}}' descriptor='
         ImageDes'/>
4    {{/index}}
5  {{/contents}}
```

Listing 1.7: medias.mustache

```
1  {{#contents}}
2    {{#next}}
3      <link id='lMoveForward{{index}}' xconnector='conBase#
         onEndStart'>
4        <bind role='onEnd' component='image{{index}}'/>
5        <bind role='start' component='image{{next}}'/>
6      </link>
7    {{/next}}
8  {{/contents}}
```

Listing 1.8: links.mustache

On mustache, were written 33 lines of code overall which leads to a *score* of **72.27%**. If all the code were removed and replaced by one single file it would have been coded 31 lines. In this case, the two removed lines are related to partials. Therefore, the slideshow made in mustache had a **73.95%** *score* in terms of the number of lines of code. Taking into account the number of instructions the *score* with and without hierarchy is **72.53%** and **74.73%**, respectively.

The Table 2 summaries the *score* achieved in the development with both two languages.

In both cases, it is seen a large reduction in the number of lines of code. More than that, this reduction is pretty much the same. A curious fact can be observed comparing the two cases. Using inheritance on both, the Jinja2 instance produced more lines in comparison to Mustache. That is because each block tag in Jinja2 generates 3 lines/instructions (one to denote the block on the parent template and two to mark its beginning and ending on the child template) plus one line for the extending tag. On the other hand, Mustache just requires the partial to be processed. Mustache separates one partial per file which eliminates the need for more tags.

Regarding what was mentioned in the previous paragraph, there is a drawback in the way Mustache works. For NCL applications that implies in more elaborated templates, the number of files grows equally to the number of partials used in the template. On Jinja2, a developer has free control of how much {% blocks %} statements he/she puts on each module.

Table 2. Slideshow score summary

Case	Jinja2	
	Number of lines	Number of instructions
w/hierarchy	72.27%	72.53%
w/o hierarchy	73.95%	74.73%
Case	Mustache	
	Number of lines	Number of instructions
w/hierarchy	69.75%	76.92%
w/o hierarchy	77.31%	82.42%

5   Final Remarks

First, we asked *How can we improve NCL development template usage?* We try to answer it by arguing that the usage of web templates in the development of NCL applications is an option to reduce typing errors. To address this question, we define the objective of **Allow web template engines processing at Ginga**.

In Sect. 4, we developed a slideshow use cases: More precisely, it was discussed how the use of Jinja2 and Mustache template languages can support the development of NCL applications. This example confirmed that web templates can reduce code-writing, independently if the metric used is the number of lines or the number of instructions in the document.

Jinja2 and Mustache template-based applications avoid code repetition and are less error-prone. Nonetheless, differently from some related works, they did not make it easier. To its authors, they still require a certain expertise in programming. In Jinja2, it is a tough task to generate the final NCL document properly indented with Jinja2. The outputted NCL document is still correct, nonetheless, it becomes less readable and not ease developers task during coding. The use of the mustache is not recommended for more complex applications, as it makes it more difficult than facilitates.

Despite targeting web development, it was not possible to conclude if web engines were suitable in the development of DTV applications. For instance, on the web, some of these engines run on the server-side, while others run on the client-side only and some can execute on both. Therefore, a second goal was defined: **Evaluate web templates usage in NCL development**. To fulfill such an objective, the NCL-formats tool was developed. It aims at assisting the development of NCL applications based on web-template languages. As discussed in Sect. 3, it can be executed as a standalone tool. We also suppose two possibilities for executing it on the client-side.

The first possibility consists of extending Ginga's parser to support templates syntax. It was extended to also handle template documents in Jinja2 or Mustache languages. In this context, the Parser receives two documents: the template and the padding. With that, the NCL-formats tool is called to process the given data and generate an NCL document ready to be played by the NCL player.

As pointed out in Sect. 3.2, this way implies modifying Ginga's standard which takes time to be approved and adopted.

Having in mind the drawbacks of the aforementioned proposal, another approach was envisaged. This solution consists of embedding NCL-format as a particular type of Lua script recognized by Ginga, NCLua. This way, an NCL Player receives a simple NCL document. The NCL-formats becomes a media element of this NCL and the required information (padding document, template document, and the engine) is passed as a property of this media element. The NCLua script gathers the passed data and calls the required web template engine. The engine fills out gaps on template document with information from padding to generate the final document. After processing, the NCLua script signalizes its ending and the final document is played.

As future work, we consider measuring the impact of our work targeting its developers. In particular, we may measure the coding time. Regarding the NCL-formats tool, it was tested against Jinja2 and Mustache template engines. However, it may be applied to process template documents in any language. Therefore, future works may enlarge it by supporting other template languages as well extend it to include other formats of NCL. Moreover, in this work we do not explore scenarios in which the template engine acts as a media such are use in Web Components. It can be used to create new types of media players. For instance, to create templates that receive an SRC file as a padding document to render subtitles.

References

1. de Albuquerque Azevedo, R.G.: LuaTPL: a simple lua-based template engine (2018). https://github.com/robertogerson/luatpl
2. Bezerra, D.H.D., Moraes, D.M.T., Filho, G.L.d.S., Burlamaqui, A.M.F., Silva, I.R.M.: Luar: a language for agile development of NCL templates and documents. In: Proceedings of the 18th Brazilian Symposium on Multimedia and the Web, WebMedia 2012, pp. 395–402. ACM, New York (2012). http://doi.acm.org/10.1145/2382636.2382718
3. Lab. TeleMídia: Ginga: The iTV middleware (2018). https://github.com/TeleMidia/Ginga
4. de Macedo Terças, L., de Sousa Moraes, D., de Sousa Lima, T., Neto, M.C.M., de Salles Soares Neto, C.: Introducing different levels of reuse to a hypermedia authoring language with macros and templates. In: Proceedings of the 24th Brazilian Symposium on Multimedia and the Web, WebMedia 2018, pp. 117–124. ACM, New York (2018). http://doi.acm.org/10.1145/3243082.3243117
5. Moraes, D.d.S., Damasceno, A.L.d.B., Busson, A.J.G., Soares Neto, C.S.: Lua2NCL: framework for textual authoring of NCL applications using Lua. In: Proceeding of 22nd Brazilian Symposium on Multimedia and the Web. ACM (2016)
6. dos Santos, J.A.F., Saade, D.C.M.: XTemplate 3.0: adding semantics to hypermedia compositions and providing document structure reuse. In: Proceedings of the 2010 ACM Symposium on Applied Computing, pp. 1892–1897. ACM (2010)

7. Soares Neto, C.S., Pinto, H.F., Soares, L.F.G.: Tal processor for hypermedia applications. In: Proceedings of the 2012 ACM Symposium on Document Engineering, DocEng 2012, pp. 69–78. ACM, New York (2012). http://doi.acm.org/10.1145/2361354.2361369

8. Soares Neto, C.S., Soares, L.F.G., de Souza, C.S.: TAL—template authoring language. J. Braz. Comput. Soc. **18**(3), 185–199 (2012). https://doi.org/10.1007/s13173-012-0073-7

9. Soares Neto, C.S., de Souza, C.S., Soares, L.F.G.: Linguagens computacionais como interfaces: um estudo com nested context language. In: Proceedings of the VIII Brazilian Symposium on Human Factors in Computing Systems, IHC 2008, pp. 166–175. Sociedade Brasileira de Computação, Porto Alegre (2008). http://dl.acm.org/citation.cfm?id=1497470.1497489

10. Terças, L., Moraes, D.d.S., Lima, T.d.S., Neto, M.C.M., Soares Neto, C.S.: Introducing different levels of reuse to a hypermedia authoring language with macros and templates. In: Proceedings of the 24th Brazilian Symposium on Multimedia and the Web. WebMedia 2018, pp. 117–124. ACM, New York (2018). http://doi.acm.org/10.1145/3243082.3243117

11. W3C: XSL Transformations (XSLT) Version 1.0 (1999). http://www.w3.org/TR/xslt. 00020

Improving a Software Framework from an Assistive Technology Application for iTV

Rafael Cardoso[1,2(✉)] , Andréia Rodrigues[1,2] , Vinícius da Costa[1,2] ,
Telmo Silva[3] , Rita Oliveira[3] , and Tatiana Tavares[1]

[1] Technological Development Center (CDTec), Federal University of Pelotas (UFPel),
Rua Gomes Carneiro, 1 - Centro, Pelotas, RS 96010-610, Brazil
{rc.cardoso,andreia.sias,viniciusdacosta,tatiana}@inf.ufpel.edu.br
[2] WeTech, Federal Institute Sul-Rio-grandense (IFSul), Praça 20 de Setembro, 455 -
Centro, Pelotas, RS 96015-360, Brazil
{rafaelcardoso,andreiasias,viniciusdacosta}@pelotas.ifsul.edu.br
[3] Digimedia, Department of Communication and Arts (DECA), University of Aveiro,
3810-193 Aveiro, Portugal
{tsilva,ritaoliveira}@ua.pt
https://wp.ufpel.edu.br/nulab/cdtec/ciencia-da-computacao/
http://www.ifsul.edu.br
http://digimedia.web.ua.pt

Abstract. TV is one of the most popular media in people's homes
around the world. Its rapid technological evolution has led to what we
today call interactive TV (iTV), a concept that extends the possibilities of its use. Despite iTV's applications to provide great advances in
the interaction with the audience, most of its features are still accessible just through conventional remote controls. This interaction device
ends up making the content inaccessible, for example, for people with
physical/cognitive limitations. Assistive Technology (AT) is a research
area focused on developing applications for this audience. An example of
an AT-based solution is IOM (*Interface Óculos Mouse*), an interaction
device that uses the head movements to access the computer. However,
to create applications that use devices (such as IOM) in different scenarios, it is necessary to provide tools that assist the development process. Reusable software structures can achieve this goal by encapsulating
essential features for using these devices. Design techniques to this type of
solution propose the development of a set of applications, under different
usage contexts, to evidence the functionalities that should be exposed by
the framework. This paper explores the survey of requirements that can
compose the IOM's software framework through IOM4TV development
and evaluation. It is an application designed to use the IOM device in the
ITV's context. Thus, the paper initially outlines the research areas' state-
of-art involved in this work. After that, the article focuses on IOM4TV's
development and testing stages. Finally, the paper highlights the requirements perceived in this context of use, which can be applied in the mod-
eling of the proposed software framework.

Keywords: Interactive TV · Assistive Technology · Framework ·
Prototyping · Software design

M. J. Absolo et al. (Eds.): jAUTI 2019, CCIS 1202, pp. 31–49, 2020.
https://doi.org/10.1007/978-3-030-56574-9_3

1   Introduction

Television (TV) is one of the most popular media streaming equipment present in homes around the world. This can be seen, for example, in Brazil, where only 2.8% of households do not have TV sets [17]. The fast technological advances of this device have led to what we know today as interactive TV (iTV). iTV uses the bidirectional communication concept, enabling user interaction with the information being displayed. This allows users to have better choices to control the experience of watching TV shows.

This new reality considerably expands the possibilities of using TV, besides its original function, allowing the development of different interaction experiences through specific software applications [42]. +TV4E platform is an iTV ecosystem application that uses TV to broadcast content about public and social services for seniors, embedding them in regular television programming [39].

Despite providing a very important service for the elderly, access to the resources available in the applications through conventional remote controls makes it difficult for part of the population to use +TV4E, specifically, people with physical or cognitive limitations. In this sense, it is estimated that one billion people suffer from some form of limitation [46]. In Brazil, according to [19], 23.9% of the population suffers from some kind of disability. Of this total, 7% of people reported motor disabilities.

Assistive Technology (AT) is the research area concerned in proposing, designing, developing, and evaluating solutions that improve people's quality of life with physical/cognitive disabilities [15]. Different AT solutions can be developed depending on the material available for its creation. Thus, an AT can range from simpler mechanisms, such as walking sticks, to devices that use sophisticated hardware and software equipment to achieve their specific purposes.

An example of an AT-based solution is the IOM project (an acronym for *Interface Óculos-Mouse*, in Portuguese). The project develops IOM, an alternative interaction device focused on people with motor limitations, which allows its users to control the mouse's actions only using head movements [26]. Initially designed to provide access to the computer for people with physical disabilities, conducting studies and developing new applications using the IOM showed its applicability to other demands, besides its original purpose.

However, for an AT, such as the IOM, to be used in different scenarios, it is interesting to make development structures available for the device specifically. These tools seek to abstract the essential resources available on the device, aiming to simplify the construction of applications that use it. This aim can be achieved by providing general reusable software structures, such as component libraries or software frameworks, for example. In this context, there are specific methodologies for the development of this general structure, by identifying properties and common features in different usage scenarios. According to this approach, the development of a set of applications in a specific domain, but in different contexts of use, helps to realize these shared characteristics.

This article explores the development process of IOM4TV, one application used to enhance the requirements that should compose the IOM framework [8].

The work presents the conception and evaluation process of this solution, high-lighting the main requirements perceived throughout this process. The requirements raised in this development cycle will be combined with subsidies from three other applications previously developed using the IOM device. The compilation of these results will allow the design of a software architecture for the development of applications aimed at people with preserved head movements, specifically using the IOM, as a case study.

The article is organized as follows: Sect. 2 presents the work's conceptual background, highlighting the contexts in which it is inserted. Section 3 describes the development of IOM4TV, as well as the +TV4E and IOM projects. Then, Sect. 4 highlights two rounds of testing on IOM4TV, using the SAM and Attrakd-iff tools. The main requirements and functionalities perceived through the evaluations carried out are highlighted in Sect. 5. Finally, Sect. 6 presents the main results achieved, besides indicating the sequence of work.

2   Conceptual Background

This section covers the essential research areas involved in this paper. First, concepts about iTV are highlighted, a research area in which the developed application is intrinsically connected. Then some Assistive Technology concepts, characteristics, and classifications are presented. Finally, software constructive aspects are explored, presenting main principles and approaches related to the architecture and software development process. In particular, we focus on issues regarding reusable software development.

2.1   Interactive TV Applications in an Assistive Context

The conventional's TV standard behavior focuses on presenting content to its viewers since, in this model, there is no interaction between people and TV. This non-participatory format depends directly on the type of content which acts as an intermediary for audience interaction, such as advertisements or films, for example [1]. Interactive TV (iTV) expands this scenario, considering a second fundamental concept in this process: interactivity [40]. This new concept, introduced in the TV usage model, involves two main elements: the form of communication; and the media environment. The combination of these concepts of interaction with TV offers users the possibility to enjoy a more appropriate experience, where the content is distributed according to their specific habits and preferences.

In turn, [33] presents an analysis of the interactive accessibility of digital TV in Brazil, considering the informal, formal, and technical levels. Based on W3C (World Wide Web Consortium) guidelines and recommendations for interactive digital TV, the article outlines a set of recommendations applicable to this scenario. GUIDE (Gentle User Interfaces for Older People), on the other hand, is a solution that takes a natural multi-modal interaction approach to provide its users with an intuitive way to control TV-based applications [12]. Using different interaction modes, GUIDE aims to be a solution that simplifies TV control for people with physical limitations. The main goal is that older people can avoid errors, or react to an incorrect interaction situation, by using a conventional remote control [13].

The work of [35] introduces a platform that aims to provide an accessible environment through custom control devices and a TV-based user home interface. The paper analyzes specific problems and individual needs faced by people with disabilities to interact with digital tools and access online services via television sets. As a result, it was possible to improve accessibility issues of existing solutions for this audience.

2.2   Assistive Technology (AT)

According to [45], in the world, about one billion people have some physical limitations. This amount of people produces a growing need for solutions that simplify their daily tasks. Assistive Technology, or AT, is a research area dedicated to designing, developing, and testing of such solutions. Using AT mechanisms refers to the beginning of human history, where pieces of sticks were used, for example, like walking sticks. Although the use of AT artifacts is old, emerging concerns about the issues covered by AT are more contemporary, aiming to include properly the individuals in society.

Formally, the term AT is originated in 1988 in the United States of America (USA). It was defined as a legal element within the country's law, known as Public Text 100–407, which makes up the American Disabilities Act (ADA) [22]. Based on the criteria set by the ADA, AT was defined as: A wide range of equipment, services, strategies, and practices designed to alleviate the functional problems encountered by individuals with disabilities [16]. Several classifications have been proposed to categorize the developed AT. One of them divides the solutions according to the cost and the functioning of the resources used in its construction [21]:

1. Low-Level AT: simple, non-electric and low-cost devices;
2. Medium-Level AT: equipment with some power supply, but that does not use computational resources; and
3. High-Level AT: solutions that use specific software and/or hardware.

Using High-Level AT, specifically, may gather several fields of study, depending on the application's requirements. Among the High-Level AT, there are solutions that invest in the development of assistive games [11,23,30] or control of specific environments, for example [31,44]. There are also works that develop solutions to provide access to computers for people with different disabilities [2,14,20,28]. Specifically, in the latter category is the IOM, an alternative interaction device for people with motor limitations [26]. Designed to be a low-cost solution, it allows control of computers through head movements.

Although initially designed for computer access, the evolution of studies, and the development of applications that use this device extend its applicability to the other demands, besides its original purpose. Thus, for an AT (like IOM) to be adopted in different contexts of use, it is interesting to provide some tools that abstract the main features and functionalities available in the device. This goal can be achieved from general reusable software structures that allow a more straightforward generation of software solutions.

2.3   Software Reuse Constructive Aspects

A software development process consists of activities set that must be performed to develop a software artifact [34]. Each of these activities, in turn, has a set of actions associated with it. Finally, each action has some tasks that identify: what needs to be completed; what artifacts to produce; quality factors; and checkpoints for tracking project progress. Although there are several software processes, all of them foresee activities for (1) Specification; (2) Project; (3) Implementation; (4) Validation; (5) Evolution to meet changes [43].

Software reuse-based is one alternative for development processes. It is directly related to the concept of creating general software structures. Such frameworks are usually cooperative classes that can be adapted or extended to build software in an application domain, reducing the implementation efforts [3,24]. There are approaches to develop such reusable software. These methodologies rely on identifying common properties and features in a family of applications [24,25,36]. The recognition of such characteristics can be achieved by developing multiple applications in a specific domain but different usage contexts. Figure 1 presents the patterns for designing reusable components, proposed by [36].

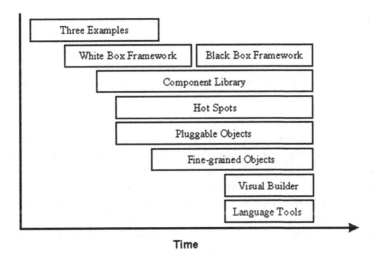

Fig. 1. Patterns for building reusable software structures.   Source: [36].

In this context, various types of software structures can be developed depending on the project's needs. For example, an Application Programming Interface

(API), a conceptual collection of methods that describe services or features provided by some application. A component library is another possible artifact, i.e., a piece of code called to run specific functions. In turn, a software framework can be viewed as a set of libraries required to perform a more broad operation. It encapsulates API behaviors into more complex implementations, allowing them to be used more flexibly through extensions, configurations, and inversions of control. Unlike libraries, a framework calls the code of the developed application, as it often provides gaps that must be filled to execute as the needs of each solution function as the application skeleton. Finally, a Software Development Kit (SDK) assists the solutions' development for a particular platform or operating system [4]. There are, of course, slight nuances about these definitions and terminologies in the literature. Nevertheless, this set of software structures encompasses the most common examples of reusable software components.

However, to create these software structures using the aforementioned techniques, the starting point is to develop at least three applications in an application domain. This work focuses on the development of a framework that simplifies the design of applications that use IOM. To achieve this goal, a series of AT development cycles using the IOM was planned. The idea is to develop four applications in different contexts of use so it is possible to identify the functionalities in each of these scenarios. Figure 2 highlights this development method.

Fig. 2. Development methodology for the IOM framework. Source: adapted from [10].

The application scopes were selected based on taxonomy derived from a systematic literature mapping on high-level AT for people with preserved head movements [9]. The aim is to gather the perceptions arising from each cycle, to build the desired reusable software structure. This paper specifically highlights the process of developing and evaluating one of these applications, called IOM4TV. The objective is to recognize requirements that can compose the framework for application development using the IOM, through the design of this AT-based application in the iTV ecosystem context.

3   An AT-Based Solution for the iTV Ecosystem

IOM4TV consists of a software solution that integrates the projects +TV4E and IOM. The goal is to use IOM as the primary form of interaction to control an interactive TV application. The development and evaluation of IOM4TV allowed us to perceive a series of features and properties that must be part of the IOM's framework. This process is detailed in the next sections of this paper.

3.1 +TV4E Project

+TV4E platform is an iTV solution conceived to turn its target audience (seniors) into users, and not just passive viewers [41]. Combining the TV with some interaction process allows distributing contents according to the specific habits and tastes of each user. This process can provide a more exciting user experience.

The idea is to provide the elderly, access to information related to public and social services. The main goal is to present relevant content to these users while they are watching TV. +TV4E prevents its users from missing the current TV program by interrupting the broadcast program so he can watch the video suggested by the platform and then return to the point where the TV show stopped. It also has a library that stores the recommended videos and uses its recommendation system to suggest this content according to the user's profile. Thus, the +TV4E platform's primary goal is to provide informational and relevant contents to the seniors while watching TV [6].

3.2 IOM Project

The current version of the IOM consists of an eyeglass frame with built-in sensors. IOM uses an accelerometer to capture the movements performed by its users. This data is used as input, then sent over a serial connection, and finally converted to cursor movements on the computer screen. Data interpretation is based on an internal communication protocol, necessary for the proper understanding and treatment of data exchanged on both sides of the communication. Figure 3 highlights IOM version 1.0, and its basic elements.

Fig. 3. IOM device main components. Source: [37].

To trigger click events, IOM version 1.0 adopts the Dwell time technique, i.e.; it simulates clicks when the device remains stationary for a configured period. The gadget is also accompanied by a setup application to customize parameters for the proper equipment use.

3.3 IOM4TV Application

IOM4TV is designed to support IOM within the +TV4E platform. In addition to the IOM, the following elements need to be interconnected:

- **TV**: The output appliance used in the interaction;
- **Set-Top Box (STB)**: Equipment responsible for transforming content into a format displayed on a TV;
- **IOM**: Alternative interaction device based on head movements; and
- **Execution Container**: A computer that connects the IOM to the TV set.

As observed in the architecture highlighted in Fig. 4, two software components were developed: +TV4E API and IOM virtual control interface. They connect all physical elements and allowing their proper communication.

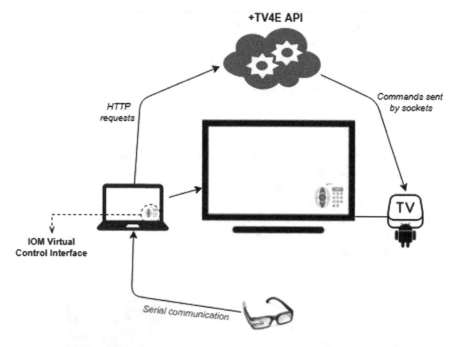

Fig. 4. IOM4TV's architecture. Source: [7].

The first component acts as a Web Service (WS), i.e., an intermediate software layer that receives data from the IOM's virtual control interface and translates it to commands on the iTV system. +TV4E API receives HTTP (Hypertext Transfer Protocol) POST calls and triggers instructions to be executed over the STB. The latter software component is a Graphical User Interface (GUI) that interacts directly with IOM. It was specifically developed to allow the interaction between IOM users and the iTV application in a simplified way. IOM4TV's basic operation works as follows. When the user clicks on any interface button, the application configures and triggers an HTTP request to WS, which performs the function associated with the clicked button. As soon as it receives this call the WS communicates with the STB, through sockets, executing the command requested by the user in the iTV application. Initially, two approaches were used to develop this IOM4TV control interface. Both methods are described below.

IOM Default Behavior-Based Prototype. The first developed interface was based on the IOM's default operating approach. In this version, the user traverses the interface using the cursor performing continuous head movements. When the user stops moving the cursor in a position (for a predefined time) the click action is triggered over the area the cursor is located.

This interface has been developed using web tools (HTML, CSS, and AJAX). Two versions of this prototype were developed, with different control interaction interfaces, which are highlighted in Fig. 5(a) and (b).

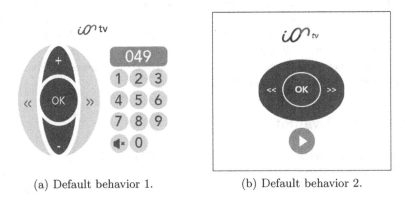

(a) Default behavior 1.   (b) Default behavior 2.

Fig. 5. IOM4TV's prototypes interfaces. Source: [7].

Event-Based Prototype. The previous prototype's evaluations motivated the development of an alternative form of interaction. The idea of this IOM4TV's version was to detect specific movement events with the IOM to simplify navigation in the application and reduce the discomfort caused by the movements necessary to use the control interface.

Thus, the IOM firmware has been adapted to detect four basic movement events: up, down, left, or right. Also, listener classes have been developed, which await movement events that trigger the functionalities that can be performed on the STB. The prototype interface, highlighted in Fig. 6, was implemented in Java.

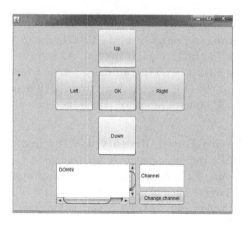

Fig. 6. Event-based prototype. Source: [7].

In this version, when moving his head the user triggers the functionality associated with each defined movement. Since the initial focus of the application is on the "OK" button on the interface, when the user moves his head to the right or left, the focus will shift to the next button available in that direction. This form of movement allows the user to move around the interface. By moving the head down, the user clicks on the button in focus.

4   IOM4TV Evaluation

Three evaluation cycles were performed with IOM4TV. The first two rounds applied to the IOM default behavior based prototype, using two assessment tools with users. The last test cycle was performed, at the implementation level, on the event-based prototype. These evaluations are detailed below.

4.1   IOM Default Behavior Based Prototype's Testing

Two rounds of user testing were performed on this prototype, using the Self-Assessment Manikin (SAM) [5] and AttrakDiff [18] tools. SAM analyzes domains that correspond to the Semantic Emotional Spatial Structure fields defined by [38]. Its evaluation scale is composed of three pictograms sets representing the domains: Valencia (satisfied/unsatisfied); Excitation (motivated/relaxed); and Control Feeling (controlled/uncontrolled) [27]. Each domain is related to a range of values, varying from 1 to 9.

In turn, AttrakDiff is an instrument to measure the attractiveness of interactive products and their relationship with the user experience. It uses 28 opposing adjectives pairs so that users can identify their perception of the tested solution. These word pairs represent the following evaluation dimensions that measure different product aspects:

- Pragmatic Quality (PQ): Related to product usability;
- Hedonic Quality Stimulation (HQ-S): Explores the product's evolutionary potential;
- Hedonic Quality Identity (HQ-I): Indicates the level of user identification with the product; and
- Attractiveness (ATT): Represents the general product quality from the user's perspective.

The purpose of using SAM and AttrakDiff in the IOM4TV evaluation was to perceive the emotions felt by the users (via SAM), and to evaluate the user experience (through AttrakDiff) during interaction with the prototype.

Each testing round involved five participants over 55, two men and three women. This number of testers was based on the theory that the best results come with no more than five users running the fewest possible activities [29]. Concerning previous participants' experiences, they all use computers daily both at home and in their work. The interaction with their computing devices occurs through conventional instruments such as a mouse, keyboard, or mouse-pad. No users have any physical/cognitive limitations.

Regarding the testing environments, in the first round, it was organized in a University computer lab, with no concerns to reproduce the context in which a user would use IOM4TV. An occupational therapist has guided the organization of the environment and the second round of tests was performed. His main concern was to make the environment attractive, like a conventional TV room, with a comfortable sofa, intimate decor, ambient lighting, and pleasant temperature.

SAM's Results. As the SAM is an instrument for assessing emotional aspects, several factors can influence users when filling out their scale. Thus, experts must analyze nuances that may occur throughout each assessment. In an initial observation, the participants considered the solution to be very satisfactory, as highlighted in Fig. 7.

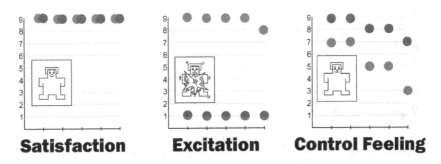

Fig. 7. SAM results: 1st round in orange; 2nd round in green. (Color figure online)

The Satisfaction aspect reached the highest score in both experiments, i.e., an average of 9 points. This positive assessment may be linked to the sense of usefulness that the elderly felt when taking part in the tests. The Excitement dimension got opposite results in the two testing rounds (reaching an average of 8.8 and 1 point, respectively). Such a result indicates the users were very anxious during the first experiment, while they were more relaxed when performing the second test. Thus, the fact that users already know the type of interaction affects this dimension.

Finally, the Feeling of Control dimension reached a median score in the first round of testing (5.4), revealing usability issues with application interaction. In the second experiment, the results show the participants were more confident using IOM4TV, reflecting on this dimension's evaluation improvement (8.2 points on average).

AttrakDiff's Results. According to AttrakDiff's results, the evaluations show that the Pragmatic and Hedonic Quality scores in the first testing round were 1.91 and 2.19, against the 2.43 and 2.51 ratings in the second series, showing a significant improvement in both aspects (see Fig. 8). The users' observations about the prototypes, allowed us to perceive problems related to both the application interface and the IOM's usability. Especially the need for more explicit visual and audible feedback (when possible). The first testing round results led to the interface evolution, as can be seen in Fig. 5(a) and (b). The main changes were related to the simplification of the control interface. Numeric buttons have been excluded to make the interface as clean as possible. The fact that there are few open channels available in Portugal led to this decision, once it is possible to navigate using back and forward buttons. Also, visual feedback has been enhanced to give users a more accurate sensation of control.

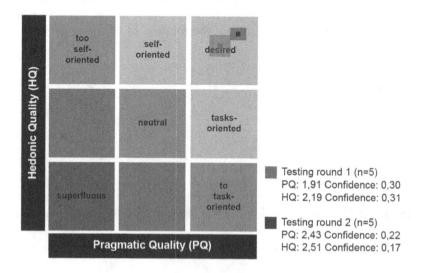

Fig. 8. AttrakDiff's Portfolio chart results.

Figure 9 highlights the average values diagram generated from the evaluations performed. The PQ values suggest that there has been a slight improvement in terms of usability. This is possibly related to the fact that users already had contact previously with the form of interaction provided by the IOM device. The HQ-I value follows this trend, showing improvement in this dimension.

Besides familiarity with the application, the welcoming environment can also impact this result. The HQ-S value remained stable, showing that the product had the same level of stimulus for the user. Finally, ATT emphasizes that the product generates a high attractiveness since it reached high levels in both evaluation rounds.

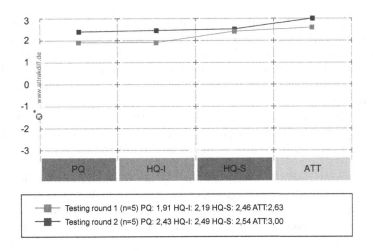

Fig. 9. AttrakDiff's average values diagram.

4.2   Event-Based Prototype's Testing

Using the navigation on the interface by responding to pre-defined head movements, instead of continuous head movement, got good results. The prototype works through a listener that is waiting to send some movements from the IOM. The interface navigation happens when the four basic movements (up, down, left, and right) are triggered by the movement of the IOM. Besides, triggering clicks through a specific movement (instead of using the Dwell time technique) showed effective results in this context.

Tests were carried out with this prototype at the development level. In this sense, three members of the research group carried out functional tests with the software under development. During the performance of these experiments, users were observed by the IOM4TV development team. No specific assessment instruments were applied at this stage since the idea was to verify the feasibility of proceeding with implementing this functionality. Thus, although the tests were carried out at the development level, this mode of operation proved promising.

In particular, the improvements are related to aspects of fatigue and discomfort reported by users when using the IOM in its standard operating mode. Besides, the event-based prototype seems to be especially suitable for situations in which the user interaction interface is small, such as the proposed virtual remote control. However, it is necessary to carry out comparative tests between the two approaches to assess the advantages and disadvantages of each one.

5   Requirements Recognized from IOM4TV

As previously highlighted, this work is part of a project that aims to develop a software framework for the IOM device. The idea is to achieve this by identifying recurrent characteristics and needs in applications that use IOM in different usage contexts. In this sense, other initiatives have already been developed using IOM as an interaction object in other scenarios, such as ambient assisted living [32] and games [11].

Specifically, in this work, the IOM4TV prototypes allowed to collect requirements related to the IOM's usage in the interactive TV scenario. Among the main points raised, it is possible to highlight the following ones.

- *Setup features*: essential tasks that shall be addressed initially, such as methods for identifying, connecting, and configuring the main functionalities available on the interaction device. It is also necessary to consider the aspects relative to the communication protocol that must exist between the device and applications;
- *Feedback*: visual feedback in the interface using enhanced colors and assistive messages. Motivated by the need to provide clear information about the functions in execution, such as changing channels or accessing the video library, for example;
- *Alternative interaction mode*: Use alternative ways to trigger specific events such as clicks. An example would be the use of voice commands for this purpose. This was a recurring request from users during the tests;
- *Application's mirroring*: Allowing the application to be inserted directly into the TV screen is an essential requirement in the iTV context. It simplifies the solution by eliminating the computer from this usage scenario;
- *Event-based functioning*: although still in the development stage, this feature was a very relevant contribution. It opens up a range of possibilities for the development of applications that may use this behavior; and
- *Clickable targets detection*: To provide methods that simplify the detection of *user click intention* when using standard device operation. This issue does not occur when the event-based mode is used. Related to identify clickable targets in the interface (usually buttons), when the cursor approaches them.

Regarding technical issues, the development of interactive interfaces using different technologies was very relevant in this work. This reinforces the understanding that a conceptual framework should be designed, regardless of the technology used in the final implementation.

Besides, concerning the development process, it is necessary to strengthen end-user participation by allowing them to cooperate more actively in the assistive solution design process. In terms of testing, critical factors such as execution environment, familiarity, and interaction tools directly influence the result achieved.

Finally, the IOM4TV design process allowed us to validate the method used for the development of reusable software structures in this project. This could be seen, since the requirements perceived in the IOM4TV development had already appeared during the development of the other three applications using IOM in other usage scenarios. In particular, the configuration and calibration aspects were recurrent in all four applications. The interaction via events was approached similarly in the game scenario application. Finally, requirements related to interaction and feedback with the IOM4TV interface also appeared at different points in the other applications created.

6   Conclusions and Future Work

This work is part of a research project that aims to propose a software framework focused on the development of AT applications for people with motor limitations. The idea is to apply development techniques to identify recurring characteristics and needs in a family of applications from a specific knowledge domain. In this sense, as highlighted, this paper specifically explores IOM4TV, one of the applications developed to recognize this software framework's requirements. Its development and evaluation process collected essential requirements related to the interactive TV scenario.

In this context, IOM4TV a software solution for controlling +TV4E application through IOM. To accomplish this integration, two software components were developed: A WS API, responsible for translating IOM actions into STB commands; And virtual control interfaces used to user interaction with the application.

Regarding the tests on the IOM4TV prototypes that are based on the IOM standard behavior, both evaluation tools, SAM and AttrakDiff, had promising results. These rounds of tests allowed to identify several points for improvements, related both to the interaction process with the IOM4TV, and usability aspects of the IOM device itself. The prototype based on response to events had relevant results, even though it was not tested with end-users.

Development-level tests have shown that the event-based approach is promising as, besides simplifying the user-application interaction, it eliminates part of the problems faced by the default operating approach. Following this work, it is expected to perform functional tests with the event-based application. Ideally, these tests should also involve end-users to get a more reliable result. Besides, this new round would make it possible to compare the modes of operation of the IOM4TV, more properly.

Regarding the research project, these prototype's development and evaluation allowed identifying a series of requirements that can be incorporated into the IOM software framework. Some features and properties raised, corroborate needs that appeared in other usage scenarios explored. Also, functionalities specifically related to the iTV ecosystem were noticed, which should integrate the framework design. This validates the development method used for proposing a reusable software framework.

The project's next step is to bring together the requirements raised from the development of IOM4TV with those already observed in other IOM's usage scenarios. Based on these elements, the aim is to design a software architecture, at the conceptual level, for the development of applications aimed at people with preserved head movements. Finally, as a case study, it is expected to implement this model as a framework for the IOM. The initial idea is to develop this structure as micro-services so that developers can select and use only the functionalities necessary to develop their specific solutions using IOM.

Acknowledgements. We are grateful for the valuable contributions made by all WeTech's researchers who contributed to this work. The authors also thank the Federal Institute Sul-Rio-grandense (IFSul) for partially financing this project. This study was financed in part by the Coordenação de Aperfeiçoamento de Pessoal de Nível Superior - Brasil (CAPES) - Finance Code 001.

References

1. Ali-Hasan, N., Soto, B.: 8 things to consider when designing interactive TV experiences (2015)
2. Antunes, R.A., Palma, L.B., Coito, F.V., Duarteramos, H., Gil, P.: Intelligent human-computer interface for improving pointing device usability and performance. In: 2016 12th IEEE International Conference on Control and Automation (ICCA), pp. 714–719 (2016)
3. Bosch, J.: Design and Use of Software Architectures: Adopting and Evolving a Product-Line Approach. Pearson Education, London (2000)
4. Bourque, P., Fairley, R.E., et al.: Guide to the Software Engineering Body of Knowledge (SWEBOK (R)): Version 3.0. IEEE Computer Society Press, Los Alamitos (2014)
5. Bradley, M.M., Lang, P.J.: Measuring emotion: the self-assessment manikin and the semantic differential. J. Behav. Ther. Exp. Psychiatry **25**(1), 49–59 (1994)
6. Caravau, H., Silva, T.: +TV4E: an interactive television platform as a support to broadcast information about social services. Libro de Aplicaciones y Usabilidad de la Televisión Digital Interactiva **11**, 17 (2016)
7. Cardoso, R., Rodrigues, A., Coelho, M., Tavares, T., Oliveira, R., Silva, T.: IOM4TV: an AT-based solution for people with motor disabilities supported in iTV. In: Abásolo, M.J., Silva, T., González, N.D. (eds.) jAUTI 2018. CCIS, vol. 1004, pp. 99–114. Springer, Cham (2019). https://doi.org/10.1007/978-3-030-23862-9_8

8. Cardoso, R., Rodrigues, A., da Costa, V., Silva, T., Oliveira, R., Tavares, T.: Enhancing the architectural requirements of an at software framework through iTV ecosystem, chap. 6, pp. 174–185. Facultad de Informática (UNLP) (2020). http://sedici.unlp.edu.ar/handle/10915/90396
9. Cardoso, R., Rodrigues, A., da Costa, V., Tavares, T.: Solutions focused on high-level assistive technology: perceptions and trends observed from a systematic literature mapping. J. Interact. Syst. 11(1) (2020). https://doi.org/10.5753/jis.2020. 789, https://sol.sbc.org.br/journals/index.php/jis/article/view/789
10. Cardoso, R.C.: Um Arcabouço de Referência para Concepção de Soluções de Tecnologia Assistiva de Alto Nível. Ph.D. thesis, Universidade Federal de Pelotas (2019)
11. Cardoso, R.C., et al.: Doce labirinto: Experiência de jogo utilizando interação baseada em movimentos da cabeça e recursos tangíveis. XV Simpósio Brasileiro de Jogos e Entretenimento Digital (2016)
12. Coelho, J., Duarte, C.: The contribution of multimodal adaptation techniques to the GUIDE interface. In: Stephanidis, C. (ed.) UAHCI 2011. LNCS, vol. 6765, pp. 337–346. Springer, Heidelberg (2011). https://doi.org/10.1007/978-3-642-21672-5_37
13. Coelho, J., Duarte, C., Biswas, P., Langdon, P.: Developing accessible TV applications. In: The Proceedings of the 13th International ACM SIGACCESS Conference on Computers and Accessibility, pp. 131–138. ACM (2011)
14. Cruz, A.J.O., et al.: New solutions for old problems: use of interfaces human/computer to assist people with visual and/or motor impairment in the use of DOSVOX and microFênix. In: Rocha, A., Correia, A.M., Costanzo, S., Reis, L.P. (eds.) New Contributions in Information Systems and Technologies. AISC, vol. 353, pp. 1073–1079. Springer, Cham (2015). https://doi.org/10.1007/978-3-319-16486-1_106
15. Disability Rights of Pennsylvania: Assistive Technology for Persons with Disabilities: An Overview (2012). https://www.disabilityrightspa.org/wp-content/uploads/2018/05/ATForPeopleWithDisabilitiesOverviewJan2018AT-1.pdf
16. Galvão Filho, T.A.: A tecnologia assistiva: de que se trata? Conexões: educação, comunicação, inclusão e interculturalidade. Porto Alegre: Redes Editora 252, 207–235 (2009)
17. Grandra, A.: Pesquisa diz que, de 69 milhões de casas, só 2,8% não tem Tv no Brasil (2018). http://agenciabrasil.ebc.com.br/economia/noticia/2018-02/uso-de-celular-e-acesso-internet-sao-tendencias-crescentes-no-brasil
18. Hassenzahl, M.: User experience(UX): towards an experiential perspective on product quality. In: Proceedings of the 20th Conference on l'Interaction Homme-Machine, pp. 11–15 (2008)
19. IBGE: Instituto Brasileiro de Geografia e Estatística - Censo Demográfico 2010, November 2010. http://www.ibge.gov.br/home/estatistica/populacao/censo2010/
20. Karpov, A., Ronzhin, A.: A universal assistive technology with multimodal input and multimedia output interfaces. In: Stephanidis, C., Antona, M. (eds.) UAHCI 2014. LNCS, vol. 8513, pp. 369–378. Springer, Cham (2014). https://doi.org/10.1007/978-3-319-07437-5_35
21. Laund, G.: Fontes de informação sobre tecnologia assistiva para favorecer a inclusão escolar de alunos com deficiências físicas e múltiplas. 2005. 224 f. Ph.D. thesis, Tese (Doutorado em Educação Especial)–Programa de Pós-Graduação em Educação Especial, Universidade Federal de São Carlos, São Carlos (2005)
22. Law, P.: Law 100–407. The Technology-Related Assistance for Individuals with Disabilities Act of (1988)

23. Lin, Y., Breugelmans, J., Iversen, M., Schmidt, D.: An adaptive interface design (AID) for enhanced computer accessibility and rehabilitation. Int. J. Hum. Comput. Stud. **98**, 14–23 (2017)

24. Linden, F.: Engineering software architectures, processes and platforms for system families - ESAPS overview. In: Chastek, G.J. (ed.) SPLC 2002. LNCS, vol. 2379, pp. 383–397. Springer, Heidelberg (2002). https://doi.org/10.1007/3-540-45652-X_24

25. Lopez-Herrejon, R.E., Linsbauer, L., Egyed, A.: A systematic mapping study of search-based software engineering for software product lines. Inf. Softw. Technol. **61**, 33–51 (2015)

26. Machado, M.B., et al.: An adaptive hardware and software based human computer interface for people with motor disabilities. IEEE Lat. Am. Trans. **17**(09), 1401–1409 (2019)

27. Mahlke, S., Minge, M.: Consideration of multiple components of emotions in human-technology interaction. In: Peter, C., Beale, R. (eds.) Affect and Emotion in Human-Computer Interaction. LNCS, vol. 4868, pp. 51–62. Springer, Heidelberg (2008). https://doi.org/10.1007/978-3-540-85099-1_5

28. Mulfari, D., Celesti, A., Fazio, M., Villari, M.: Human-computer interface based on IoT embedded systems for users with disabilities. In: Giaffreda, R., et al. (eds.) IoT360 2014. LNICSSITE, vol. 150, pp. 376–383. Springer, Cham (2015). https://doi.org/10.1007/978-3-319-19656-5_50

29. Nielsen, J., Landauer, T.K.: A mathematical model of the finding of usability problems. In: Proceedings of the INTERACT'93 and CHI'93 Conference on Human Factors in computing systems, pp. 206–213. ACM (1993)

30. Ossmann, R., Thaller, D., Nussbaum, G., Veigl, C., Weiß, C.: Making the playstation 3 accessible with AsTeRICS. In: Miesenberger, K., Karshmer, A., Penaz, P., Zagler, W. (eds.) ICCHP 2012. LNCS, vol. 7382, pp. 443–450. Springer, Heidelberg (2012). https://doi.org/10.1007/978-3-642-31522-0_67

31. Paul, B., Marcombes, S., David, A., Struijk, L.N.A., Le Moullec, Y.: A context-aware user interface for wireless personal-area network assistive environments. Wirel. Pers. Commun. **69**(1), 427–447 (2013)

32. Peroba, J.A., et al.: An IoT application for home control focused on assistive technology. In: Anais Estendidos do XXIII Simpósio Brasileiro de Sistemas Multimídia e Web, pp. 119–122. SBC (2017)

33. Piccolo, L.S.G., Melo, A.M., Baranauskas, M.C.C.: Accessibility and interactive TV: design recommendations for the Brazilian scenario. In: Baranauskas, C., Palanque, P., Abascal, J., Barbosa, S.D.J. (eds.) INTERACT 2007. LNCS, vol. 4662, pp. 361–374. Springer, Heidelberg (2007). https://doi.org/10.1007/978-3-540-74796-3_34

34. Pressman, R., Maxim, B.: Engenharia de Software-8ª Edição. McGraw Hill Brasil (2016)

35. Rivas-Costa, C., Anido-Rifón, L., Fernández-Iglesias, M.J., Gómez-Carballa, M.A., Valladares-Rodríguez, S., Soto-Barreiros, R.: An accessible platform for people with disabilities. Int. J. Hum. Comput. Interact. **30**(6), 480–494 (2014)

36. Roberts, D., Johnson, R.: Evolving frameworks. Pattern Lang. Program Des. **3** (1996)

37. Rodrigues, A.S., et al.: Evaluation of the use of eye and head movements for mouse-like functions by using IOM device. In: Antona, M., Stephanidis, C. (eds.) UAHCI 2016. LNCS, vol. 9738, pp. 81–91. Springer, Cham (2016). https://doi.org/10.1007/978-3-319-40244-4_9

38. Scherer, K.R.: The nature and dynamics of relevance and valence appraisals: theoretical advances and recent evidence. Emot. Rev. **5**(2), 150–162 (2013)
39. Silva, C.: Geração automática de conteúdo audiovisual informativo para seniores. Master's thesis, Universidade de Aveiro, Aveiro, Portugal (2017)
40. Silva, T.: Identificação de utilizadores seniores em televisão interativa. Ph.D. thesis, Universidade de Aveiro, Aveiro, Portugal (2014)
41. Silva, T., Abreu, J., Antunes, M., Almeida, P., Silva, V., Santinha, G.: +TV4E: interactive television as a support to push information about social services to the elderly. Procedia Comput. Sci. **100**, 580–585 (2016)
42. Silva, T., Reis, L., Hernández, C., Caravau, H.: Building informative audio-visual content automatically: a process to define the key aspects. In: Proceedings of the 6th Iberoamerican Conference on Applications and Usability of Interactive TV (jAUTI 2017), pp. 132–143 (2017)
43. Sommerville, I., et al.: Engenharia de Software, vol. 9. Pearson Prentice Hall, São Paulo (2011)
44. Tripathy, D., Raheja, J.L.: Design and implementation of brain computer interface based robot motion control. FICTA **2**, 289–296 (2014)
45. WHO: Disability and rehabilitation: World report on disability (2017). https://www.who.int/disabilities/world_report/2011/report.pdf
46. World Health Organization: World report on disability (2019). https://www.who.int/disabilities/world_report/2011/report.pdf

Second Screen and Crossmedia

Smartly: A TV Companion App to Deliver Discount Coupons

Telmo Silva[✉], Pedro Almeida, Bernardo Cardoso[iD], Rita Oliveira[iD], Ana Cunha, and Cláudia Ribeiro

DigiMedia, University of Aveiro, Campus Universitário Santiago, 3810-193 Aveiro, Portugal
{tsilva,almeida,bernardoc,ritaoliveira,cunha.filipa.ana,
ribeiro.csa}@ua.pt

Abstract. Commonly, users' attention is divided between multiple devices like the consumption of television content and the use of another device, such as smartphones. In this case, users tend to use mobile phones while ads are being advertised. The Smartly project aims to explore the potential o using multiple screens to enhance the TV experience by allowing users to receive on their smartphones promotion coupons related to the television content they watched. Following the development of the backend system and the mobile application, the project advanced for a test phase. During this phase, several data gathering techniques were used, such as questionnaire surveys, interviews, and direct observation of users interacting with the application. The user experience results allowed to get the instrumental, non-instrumental, and emotional impact of the application. To assess the system's user experience, the SUS scale, the AttrakDiff questionnaire, and the SAM scale were used. The results obtained through interviews allowed to find that the Smartly user experience was positive and met the main application goals.

Keywords: Interactive television · Smartphone · Second screen · Notifications · User experience · User interface

1 Introduction

Currently, we are facing an increase in the use of mobile devices while watching television content [1]. The user is exposed to an endless number of stimuli that can lead to an information overload. Thus, to get users' attention it is necessary to offer them services that meet their needs, with personalized experiences. Considering this trend, the Smartly project aims to expand the range of services offered to the consumer, trying to capture their attention through complementary information between the television and the smartphone. Thus, Smartly aims to fill this gap by encouraging consumers to watch television ads providing them with related promotional coupons. To achieve this, a set of tools capable of triggering notifications, which are associated with the TV content, were developed. When a specific notification appears on the television screen, the user is invited to press the yellow button of the remote triggering an invitation to use a mobile app. Once installed, the mobile application allows users to receive, manage and use promotional coupons related with watched TV adds.

M. J. Abásolo et al. (Eds.): jAUTI 2019, CCIS 1202, pp. 53–66, 2020.
https://doi.org/10.1007/978-3-030-56574-9_4

2   Theoretical Context

This paper reports on the Smartly research project that incorporates an ecosystem in which an interactive television (iTV) application and a mobile application are part. Therefore, the concepts of iTV and smartphone are fundamental in the structure and design of the conceptual framework of this work.

iTV combines enriched TV content with the existence of a return channel [2] allowing applications to have interactivity, enhancing their ability to meet user needs. The second-screen concept enriches the TV viewing experience, because users can benefit from mobile applications in parallel with the usage of TV screen [3]. According to a Nielsen's survey [4] about TV viewing and digital device usage, 35% of respondents look up or shop for products and services after they were advertised on TV. Notifications appear as a connection link of this technological ecosystem: iTV and smartphone. They serve as a link [5], allowing users to be warned that they have new information available [6] and can be transmitted in several forms (visual, audio or haptic) [7]. Although notifications are considered beneficial to user, they are also considered a great source of distraction [8]. However, this is not a reason to be deactivated, users give them great value because without cognitive effort, it is easy to obtain relevant information [9].

According to [10], about 52% of smartphone owners (this number continues to increase) want to be connected to their personal device as well as to television, creating a multi-screen scenario. In that sense, it was necessary to find and describe examples of applications allowing this kind of interactivity, but also applications that notify users in several devices simultaneously.

Following, a set of examples of applications is listed and a brief description and the explanation of main features and functionalities, strengths and weaknesses are presented.

LG webOS TVNotify - The purpose of this application is to enable users to view notifications (for example, from missed calls, messages, emails, or be related to the user's social networks) on television that commonly are only be displayed on smartphones, So, users do not need to always be close to the smartphone. It offers privacy control settings allowing certain personal information not to be transmitted on television and give the user the power to choose which kind of notification he prefers to see. More recently, the application has allowed to be added to a black list from which we do not want to receive notifications on television [11].

Notifications for Fire TV - Like the previously mentioned application, this allows the user to forward notifications received on the mobile phone to the television. Other features have been added like the ability to make phone calls, send images from other applications, take screenshots, and quickly search for other applications and the ability to customize the notification. The great advantage of this application is to allow privacy mode for specific applications [12].

2ndVision - This application automatically syncs a mobile application with the TV content (using audio fingerprint), showing on the tablet complementary content related to what is being shown on the TV (name of the actors, a brand of a car, information on a location seen on the TV show, among others). The user can find all the information previously mentioned in the feed, filter the contents by a certain category (e.g.: location, weather, etc.) and store them for later use. There is an agenda that allows users to specify, according to their preferences, the programs they want to see later. The application allows also to create notifications, letting users to receive content alerts. The user may also classify the additional information through the rating and share it using e-mail or social networks. All extra content is gathered and presented to the user due to audio recognition features, namely audio fingerprint [13].

Sony Notify BRAVIA is an Android application that, like the applications mentioned above, allows users to choose which of their personal applications can forward the alert to the TV set, as well as to change the privacy settings (between basic and advanced). If they are on the same wi-fi network as the television, a pairing between the smartphone and the Sony TV can be done and notifications can be forward from the smartphone to the TV set. As differentiating factors, this application allows users to view the history of the notifications received by TV and all people on the same Wi-Fi network can connect to it, creating multiple connections [14].

3 Smartly Project

The Smartly project is a partnership between Aveiro University and Altice Labs, aiming to create a set of tools capable of promoting television ads consumption, using mobile devices. To promote this, it offers a feature that allows the user to receive a notification, while watching TV, to install a mobile application. After installing and signing into the application, whenever a user has the TV tuned on the channel that shows an enriched ad, the notification is displayed int the TV set and the user will receive a notification on the mobile application with an offer related to the television content (the ad).

To create this ecosystem, it was necessary to develop a network between a set of components, such as: Content Recognition Engine, MEO Infrastructure (MEO is the IPTV service from Altice Labs), Smartly application, Smartly Database and Smartly TV application. These components and their connections are represented through the Smartly system architecture diagram (Fig. 1).

3.1 General Architecture

The system architecture comprises multiple parts. The "backend" part uses a couple of API's to allow to manage notifications in the Smartly database and in the Smartly mobile application. This "backend" part is also responsible for checking the necessary requirements for receiving a notification (through Engine Content Recognition and MEO Infrastructure) and to display it in the television (through Smartly TV application). In the "frontend" part a web interface for the backend management (Smartly Web interface) and a mobile application (Smartly mobile application) where user can see and manage his coupons were developed.

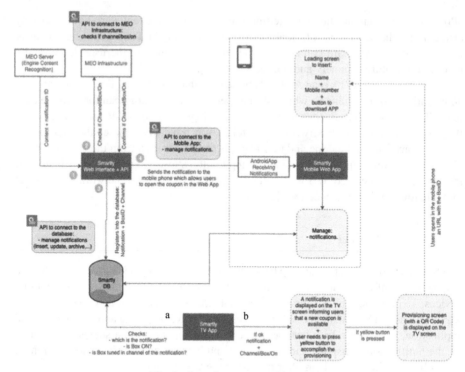

Fig. 1. Smartly system architecture

The whole notification process comprises different steps that are shown in Fig. 1 and described here.

1. The Content Recognition Engine constantly analyses if the transmitted content has associated coupons. When the system detects that such a content is being emitted, for which there are associated coupons, a notification is sent to the Web interface API, and the next steps are triggered.
2. In the MEO Infrastructure it is checked if the boxes are active and, if so, if they are tuned in the channel where the content is being broadcasted.
3. If the set-top box is active and is tuned to the channel where the content is being broadcasted, this information is communicated back to the API Web Interface that inserts, into the database, information about the notification, the Set-top Box ID and the channel.
4. A notification is sent to the smartphone allowing users to open the coupon in Smartly Mobile App.

The Smartly TV App will make regular requests to the database to check if there are new notifications to show (a). After detecting that exists a new notification, a message appears on the television screen indicating the existence of a new offer and informs the user that is necessary to press the yellow button on the remote to perform the provisioning (b). Provisioning is the procedure that associates mobile phones to a specific set-top box

(STB). This procedure is only necessary in the first use or when the user wants to associate a smartphone with a STB (it is possible to have one smartphone associated to n STB). After completing the provisioning, the coupons will be automatically sent to all associated smartphones. If the yellow button is pressed (on the remote of the STB), the provisioning screen appears with a QR Code, which redirects the user (through a URL with the Box ID) to an interface requiring: i) The name of the user; ii) The mobile number to identify uniquely the user; iii) Download the application throughout Google Play store.

In the second step, when the user enters his mobile number and clicks "Next", the database is updated, to associate the mobile number with the previously registered Box ID. Following the installation, the user is presented with a welcome screen and is required to authorize the necessary permissions for its full operation, namely the access to the mobile number. This permission will register the users to receive notifications, because is necessary to check in the database which Box ID is associated with that specific mobile device. Smartly Mobile App allows the user to not only view their coupons, but also manage the notifications. The Web Interface API, the Mobile App and the TV App interact with the Smartly database, either to save user information, boxes and mobile numbers, as well as user management (mobile number, Box ID, notifications, categories, etc.), notifications and relationships between users and notifications. It should be noted that notifications sent to users' smartphones are always made according to their customized preferences (they can select the categories of notifications they want to receive throughout mobile application).

3.2 Mobile Application

The Smartly mobile application allows users to manage their coupons and preferences. Figure 2 and Fig. 3 depicts the main screens of the application, where four menu sections are visible: "Home", "Coupons", "Help", "Definitions".

Fig. 2. Smartly mobile app

The "Home" (Início) screen is the application landing page and shows the new coupons, the expired ones and the number of favorite coupons the user has.

When the user chooses the "Coupons" (Cupões) menu item he has access to the "Categories" (Categorias) page, where the coupons are listed by categories where the user has the possibility to search for a specific coupon using the search box on the top of the screen. He can also add or remove a coupon from the favorites or simply see more details about it.

In the "Help" (Ajuda) menu item the user will find the application tutorial. In the "Definitions" (Definições) menu item the user can choose from which categories the user wants to receive notifications, manage the Set-top boxes the user is linked to, turn on/off notifications and see the privacy policy.

Fig. 3. Smartly mobile app

4   Evaluation Methodology

Aiming to provide users a rich experience in this ecosystem, it is mandatory to test solutions with the target audience. This can be achieved through tests that consider user experience (UX) and interface design. Several UX definitions are available but [15] they as being associated with the experience and interactivity between the user and a technological device, in other words, are the perceptions and responses that emerge from the interaction between an individual and a technological device during product, system or service usage. It becomes difficult to define this concept, since there are several perspectives on it. However, this is a consequence of three variables: the user's way of thinking and acting; how the system was developed; and the context in which it was experienced [16]. As for interaction design, according to [17], it covers four main practices: identifying needs and establishing requirements; develop alternative design to meet certain requirements; build interactive versions of the design developed so they can be communicated and benchmarked; and to evaluate what was developed during the process.

The user experience (UX) is still a difficult concept to define because it is associated with diffuse and dynamic concepts: emotional, affective and aesthetic variables. The UX analysis is also very versatile because it can focus on an individual interaction between the user and the application or on multiple interactions of countless users with one or several services [18]. In addition to the definition of UX it is also important to identify the evaluation methods of this concept. [19] emphasizes that if the evaluated product has already been available to users a few months ago allows a better evaluation of the product by them since they have already had the opportunity to try it. On the other hand, when evaluating a prototype, especially on paper, it becomes more difficult to provide the actual context in which the product is inserted to the user. However, sooner UX is evaluated in a product or service, more successful it will be since errors and constraints arising from user feedback can be bypassed in earlier stages, which will be noticeable to users later in use of the product in the daily basis [20].

The methodology used in the tests is divided into four phases (Fig. 4).

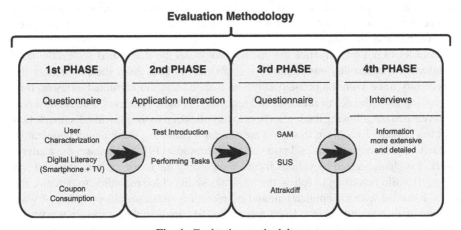

Fig. 4. Evaluation methodology

In the first phase, the participant characterization was made using a questionnaire based survey, allowing researchers to organize and assemble data faster and more rigorously. In this survey, the user was questioned through multiple-choice questions (with single and multiple answers) and open-ended questions about the personal information (gender, age, literacy, etc.), digital literacy as well as television and smartphone usage habits (including the use of digital discount coupons).

The second phase included a short introduction about the Smartly project and then the user is invited to watch TV while interacting with the mobile application. Researchers asked participants to perform thirteen specific tasks in the Smartly mobile application while watching a TV video that simulates the TV broadcast (the video includes news programs and commercial breaks where a notification informing that a new coupon is available appears).

After finishing the interaction, the third phase of the methodology was started, in which the user must fill out a new questionnaire survey to evaluate the UX/UI.

Finally, the fourth phase of this methodology included an interview to obtain information about user overall impressions.

In the case of Smartly, SUS (System Usability Scale), Attrakdiff and Self-Assessment Manikin (SAM) were used to evaluate the user experience. SUS questionnaire was used to measure instrumental qualities such as effectiveness, efficiency, satisfaction [21]. It consists of a ten-item questionnaire with five response options (likert scale) for participants, from strongly agree to strongly disagree. Attrakdiff questionnaire was mainly used to determine non-instrumental qualities such as aesthetics and visual identity of the application [22]. This instrument is based on semantic differentials and consists of 28 seven-step items whose poles are opposite adjectives (e.g. "good - bad"). Each set of adjective items is ordered into a scale of intensity. SAM scale helped to analyze the user's emotional reactions, such as pleasure, arousal, and dominance over the application [23]. The SAM scale is based in three diagrams in which the first measures the level of satisfaction between happy and sad, the second measures the motivation from excited/enthusiastic to calm/boring, and the third measures submissive to powerful control. The fact that the range of possibilities varies between opposite feelings allows users to state the level of intensity over each emotion as well as to see whether it has been positive, negative or neutral.

In order to put into practice this methodology and the mentioned scales, the tests occurred in a controlled environment – a laboratory. This gives the researchers the opportunity to be with the participants in an isolated and uninterrupted moment, thus controlling the influence of the context. Frequently, in these moments, a direct observation is carried out allowing the researchers to pay attention to the individual's interaction with the system. To achieve this there are several techniques: think aloud, cooperative evaluation, protocol analysis and post-talk walkthroughs [19]. In this case, the analysis protocol is characterized by various forms of recording the users' actions: i) pencil and paper; ii) audio recording to follow the think aloud; iii) video recording to perceive the users' behavior with the application; and iv) recording of data/problems/notes of what is going on throughout the test. Users were asked to comment their experience with the system after the interaction but with the opportunity to resume the use of the application while they were being questioned by the researchers about the application. This method, called Post-talk walkthroughs, is used when the tasks requested by the researchers are demanding and do not allow verbalization at the moment of interaction by the user, like in the case of this work [19] registration.

5   Results Analysis

After completing the tests with the users, data from both questionnaire and interviews were analyzed.

Most of the subjects who participated in the study were between 18 to 29 years old (13), three (3) participants were between 30 to 39 and five (5) were between 40 to 49.

5.1   Questionnaires

Characterization
According to the participants characterization questionnaire, most of the subjects do not

watch TV for more than two hours a day and, when they do, it is at night. When asked what action they took when advertising is announced, the responses were not consistent, because height (8) participants answered "I change to another channel," six (6) said "I don't change channels, but I don't pay attention to it" and six referred "Depends on advertising", and no participant answered "I see because it might be interesting". These answers were somewhat disappointing, however, when participants were asked whether they would make an effort to see advertising if the discounts worth it or if they liked it, participants responded positively, saying that this could be the reason to change their attitude. Regarding the categories most significant for consumers, "technology" was the one that got the most interest from the participants with fourteen (14) selections. Additionally, they also found other relevant categories: "supermarket" (5), "fashion" (6), "health and wellbeing" (5), "home and decoration" (7), and "leisure/travel" (9).

When participants were asked if they use other technological gadgets while watching TV and which are they, fourteen (14) subjects mentioned smartphone, four (4) said tablet, two (2) referred computer, and four (4) participants did not use any device. When participants use the smartphone, they handle it during advertising (8), to search for additional information (9), to entertain themselves (11), and to talk with others (2).

In contrast, participants do not give clear feedback about receiving discount notifications on the smartphone, since nine (9) subjects answered that they would not like to gain discount coupons and eleven (11) said they would be receptive to get coupons. The participants who responded affirmatively were also asked to justify their answer and some reasons were: "The smartphone is the device I pay most attention to and therefore it is the most convenient spot to see and use the notifications" and "It is the easier way to immediately access to new discounts".

When questioned if they would be willing to receive notifications about advertising on their smartphone, half of the users answers positively and the other half negatively. The participants who gave a positive answer, indicated justifications such as: "Because sometimes I may not be with 100% attention on the TV screen", "It would serve as a reminder", and "To facilitate information retrieval".

The use of discount coupons by the participants varies widely. Most of the subjects (11) reports that they use them rarely, and three (3) users use coupons several times a month. The options "once a month", "several times a week", and "once a week" only had two selections each. Most of the participants (18) had already used digital coupons rather than paper coupons (2), according to users, because "It does not take up space and it is a more environmentally friendly way", "Digital coupons are easier to store and organize", and "Sustainability reasons". The same reasons mentioned above should have led participants to opt for coupons in QR Code format, but only seven (7) subjects select this option, and vouchers got the same amount of responses. Barcode and alphanumeric coupons had three selections each. These types of coupons are the most popular formats in stores and supermarket chains, the resistance to change in adopting digital formats can explain this fact.

UX/UI Tests
Regarding the evaluation of user experience, the research team used the SAM, SUS, and Attrakdiff questionnaires. The results are listed in Table 1 and discussed in the next paragraphs.

Table 1. Application score according to the SUS, SAM, AttrakDiff instruments

Instrumental qualities	Non-instrumental qualities			Emotional reactions			
SUS (0 to 100)	AttrakDiff (−3 to 3)				SAM (1 to 5)		
	PQ	HQ-S	HQ-I	ATT	S	A	D
82,6	1,34	0,51	1,15	1,81	4,23	3,64	4,63

The SAM questionnaire allowed to measure the user emotional responses when interact with the application. Three factors were measured with the 5-point rating scale version: satisfaction (1 - low satisfaction, 5 - high satisfaction), arousal (1 - low motivation, 5 - high motivation) and dominance (1 - low control, 5 - high control) [23]. The results in the test were: satisfaction = 4.23; arousal = 3.64; and dominance = 4.63. Considering this, it was noticeable that the feedback and the results of the SAM depict a general satisfaction of the users, although the motivation could be greater (that is why several extra functionalities were proposed). Regarding control, the obtained value was positive and the users feedback showed that in most features the user felt confident and with control of the action, even though there are some improvements to be made.

The SUS questionnaire, as referred in the methodology, is used to evaluate the overall usability of the system. Through the answers given, on a scale from 1 to 5 [21], the researchers perform their analysis by subtracting one from the answers to the odd questions and, in pair questions subtracting five the user response. After that, the values are then the result multiplied by 2,5. After that, the researchers obtained the amount 82.6, which is included in the fourth and last quartile of this scale rating (Fig. 5).

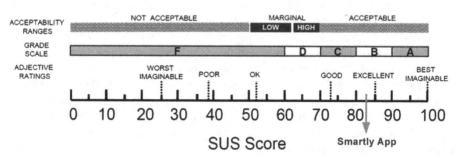

Fig. 5. Representation of the SUS results of Smartly app

Attrakdiff allows getting three types of results: the resulting portfolio, the mean value diagram, and the description of word pairs [22]. The result portfolio measures, along the vertical axis of the visualization, the hedonic quality (HQ), while the horizontal axis displays the pragmatic quality (PQ). According to the image generated by the evaluation of Smartly application (Fig. 6), this product has a pragmatic quality of 1,34 (with 0,23 of confidence) and hedonic quality of 0,83 (with 0,25 of confidence).

Portfolio-presentation

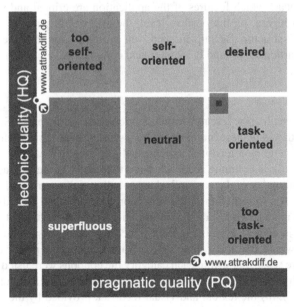

Fig. 6. Result diagram of Smartly App - portfolio of results

The diagram of average values measures the pragmatic quality (PQ), hedonic quality (HQ), both identity (HQ-I) and stimulation (HQ-S) as well as attractiveness (ATT) (Fig. 7). Thus, it shows that the four values are above 0 (on a scale of −3 to 3), where stimulation is the lowest (HQ-S: 0,51) and attractiveness is the highest (ATT: 1,81).

Diagram of average values

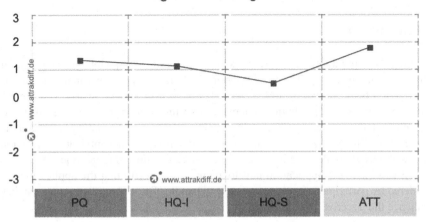

Fig. 7. Result diagrams of Smartly App - average values

Finally, considering the word pairs, it is important need to pay attention to results as these can indicate which features of the application are critical and which are well resolved. In this regard, on the positive level, the app was considered very practical, manageable, well structured, complete, and well presented. On the other hand, on the negative level, participants found it common and complicated.

5.2 Interviews

After the questionnaires, the research team interviewed the participants. Some important insights were gathered in these moments. The most relevant are listed below subdivided in two categories: common feedback and unusual feedback.

Some of the user's common feedback were related to: i) the interaction with the coupons ("The auto play of the carousels does not allow full control and the transitions are too slow.", "The information on each coupon has too many clickable steps. This becomes annoying and, in addition, the information becomes redundant."); ii) the way coupons search is done ("Why is there only the possibility of searching in the "all" coupons tab? I would like to be able to search in the entire menu for coupons.", "It would make more sense that within each category the coupons were listed as in the "all" coupon tab. It would be more consistent, and it would be easier and quicker to find a specific coupon."); iii) the textual and visual feedback provided by the application ("I think the coupon validation date is missing at the home menu. For me that is an essential piece of information.", "I realized which was the bookmarks button and how to use it, and I was not surprised by the plus or minus symbol, despite being accustomed with the state color differentiation.").

Alongside, the unusual ones were: i) "the coupon expiration date should always visible"; ii) "the application should allow the user to choose, in each category, how he wants to view coupons - list or carousel". Although they can be obvious aspects, they were not implemented at the development stage by the researchers in order to simplify the user interface and to maintain application consistency.

6 Conclusions

With the increasing adoption of second-screen devices as complementary applications while users are watching TV, the importance of finding solutions that can balance user attention between two or more screens becomes even more relevant. The Smartly application proposes a distribution scheme of discount coupons that follows this issue.

The adopted methodology to evaluate the Smartly user experience was divided into 4 phases: user characterization questionnaire, interaction with the application, questionnaires with UX/IU scales and interviews. This strategy allowed to get relevant data for the next phases of the application development and to verify that the application was considered by participants intuitive and easy to handle. These important inputs can help to enhance the advertising efficiency.

References

1. Clement, J.: Second screen usage - statistics & facts. Statista (2019). https://www.statista. com/topics/2531/second-screen-usage/. Accessed 23 Jul 2019
2. Barth, F.J., Satoshi Gomi, E.S.: Uma arquitetura para criação de interfaces adaptativas para televisão interativa (2004)
3. Geerts, D., Leenheer, R., De Grooff, D., Negenman, J., Heijstraten, S.: In front of and behind the second screen: viewer and producer perspectives on a companion app. In: Proceedings of the ACM International Conference on Interactive Experiences for TV and Online Video, pp. 95–102 (2014)
4. The Nielsen Company: The Nielsen Total Audience Report: Q2 2018, US (2018)
5. Gameiro, F.: Platform of Advertising and Push Notifications for Mobile Apps, Coimbra (2014)
6. Mehrotra, A., Musolesi, M., Hendley, R., Pejovic, V.: Designing content-driven intelligent notification mechanisms for mobile applications. In: Proceedings of the 2015 ACM International Joint Conference on Pervasive and Ubiquitous Computing - UbiComp 2015, pp. 813–824 (2015)
7. Iqbal, S.T., Bailey, B.P.: Effects of intelligent notification management on users and their tasks. In: Proceeding of the Twenty-Sixth Annual CHI Conference on Human Factors in Computing Systems - CHI 2008, p. 93 (2008)
8. Pielot, M., Church, K., de Oliveira, R.: An in-situ study of mobile phone notifications. In: Proceedings of the 16th International Conference on Human-Computer Interaction with Mobile Devices & Services - MobileHCI 2014, pp. 233–242 (2014)
9. Iqbal, S.T., Horvitz, E.: Notifications and awareness: a field study of alert usage and preferences. In: Proceedings of the 2010 ACM Conference on Computer Supported Cooperative Work - CSCW 2010, p. 27 (2010)
10. Smith, A., Boyles, J.L.: The Rise of the "Connected Viewer" (2012). https://www.pewint ernet.org/2012/07/17/the-rise-of-the-connected-viewer/
11. Google Play: LG webOS TV Notify (2019)
12. Google Play: Notifications for Fire TV (2019). https://play.google.com/store/apps/details? id=de.cyberdream.firenotifications.google
13. Abreu, J., Almeida, P., Silva, T.: A UX evaluation approach for second-screen applications. In: Abásolo, M.J., Perales, F.J., Bibiloni, A. (eds.) jAUTI/CTVDI -2015. CCIS, vol. 605, pp. 105–120. Springer, Cham (2016). https://doi.org/10.1007/978-3-319-38907-3_9
14. Google Play: Notify BRAVIA (2019). https://play.google.com/store/apps/details?id=com. sony.sid.notifybravia&hl=pt_PT
15. International Organization for Standardization: Ergonomics of Human-System Interaction — Part 110: Dialogue principles. ISO (2006). https://www.iso.org/obp/ui/#iso:std:iso:9241:-110:ed-1:v1:en. Accessed 28 Nov 2018
16. Hassenzahl, M., Tractinsky, N.: User experience - a research agenda. Behav. Inf. Technol. 25(2), 91–97 (2006)
17. Preece, J., Rogers, Y., Sharp, H.: Inter, Action Design Beyond Human-Computer Interaction. Wiley, New York (2002)
18. Law, E., Roto, V., Vermeeren, A.P.O.S., Kort, J., Hassenzahl, M.: Towards a shared definition of user experience. In: Proceeding of the Twenty-Sixth Annual CHI Conference Extended Abstracts on Human Factors in Computing Systems - CHI 2008, p. 2395 (2008)
19. Figueiredo, C.F.P.: A sensibilidade ao contexto na utilização de aplicações móveis. Universidade de Aveiro (2011)
20. Roto, V., Ketola, P., Huotari, S.: User experience evaluation in Nokia. In: CHI, p. 5 (2008)
21. Brooke, J.: SUS: a retrospective. J. Usability Stud. 8(2), 29–40 (2013)

22. UID-GMBH: Attrakdiff. http://www.attrakdiff.de/. Accessed 23 Jul 2019
23. Bynion, T.-M., Feldner, M.T.: Self-Assessment Manikin. In: Zeigler-Hill, V., Shackelford, T. (eds.) Encyclopedia of Personality and Individual Differences, p. 3. Springer, Cham (2017). https://doi.org/10.1007/978-3-319-28099-8

Mobility in Crossmedia Systems, the Design Challenges that Need to Be Addressed

Alcina Prata[1](✉) [ID] and Teresa Chambel[2] [ID]

[1] Superior School of Business Management (ESCE), Polytechnic Institute of Setúbal, Setúbal, Portugal
Alcina.prata@esce.ips.pt
[2] LASIGE, Faculty of Sciences, University of Lisbon, Lisbon, Portugal
mtchambel@ciencias.ulisboa.pt

Abstract. A few years ago, the proliferation of new devices with improved technological characteristics and interfaces, associated with better communication features and services design, conducted to a change in the viewing paradigm. In fact, users started using devices simultaneously. This convergence tendency, which resulted in the use of different devices as part of the same crossmedia system, has created new opportunities to support a multiplicity of contexts of use, as for instance, the ones associated with learning. This paper addresses the effective design of crossmedia systems to generate personalized informal learning contents from iTV, PC and mobile devices with a special focus on mobile devices. It presents the opportunities and challenges of the inclusion of mobile devices on this crossmedia systems, as well as the design challenges that need to be addressed in order to correctly add the mobility feature. The system that was designed to illustrate our research, named eiTV, generates a crossmedia personalized informal learning content, through the form of a web-based content, which provides extra information about users' selected topics of interest while watching a specific video. The web content may be generated and accessed through iTV, PC and mobile devices and, depending on the users' needs, viewed immediately or stored for latter view, individually or simultaneously, also from iTV, PC and mobile devices. The system was designed and evaluated based on cognitive and affective aspects that influence the user experience. An evaluation was carried out with high fidelity prototypes with a special focus on mobile devices. The achieved results were very good considering that they helped rethink our mobile related assumptions and they showed that the integration of mobile devices on the system was a success.

Keywords: Mobility · Crossmedia · iTV · Design challenges · Learning environment · Informal learning

1 Introduction

The proliferation of new devices able to support human activities across a range of contextual settings [1] is one of the main motivations for media integration in what is designated as Crossmedia or Transmedia environments [2]. These environments, based in the integration and co-existence of various media technologies with an integrated and specific purpose, are becoming increasingly popular due to their flexibility and mobility. They create new opportunities for the generalization of communicational practices, as those associated with formal and informal learning and information access, which are becoming more relevant considering the importance of lifelong learning [3] and the pervasive nature of media technologies and devices.

Video is a very rich medium to support learning, and TV, PC and, more recently, mobile devices are privileged ways to access it. Through structure and interaction, these devices can open the door to flexible environments that can access video and integrate it with different media, accessible from different devices, adequate to support different cognitive modes and learning processes in several contexts. In spite of their valuable potential to create rich and flexible environments, the design of these crossmedia systems faces some challenges that may affect their effective use. Some of the proposed systems failed because too much effort was put into technical details, leaving behind crossmedia conceptual aspects such as interaction and service design based on: cognitive processes, usability, user experience, contextualization, continuity, media affordances, and device characteristics.

Our main concern is to focus also and mainly on these aspects, while studying and understanding this emerging paradigm, where research has not been complete [1, 4]. The application that has been designed and developed to illustrate our research and has been through an evolution process of 3 generations of prototypes, all ranging from low to high fidelity prototypes, was named eiTV. This name was chosen because it was considered that the 'e' brings a broader 'web perspective' to the interactive television (iTV). The eiTV third generation prototypes, presented in this paper, were the richer ones in terms of devices and functionalities involved, which increased to match a more flexible perspective. These third generation prototypes fully support mobile devices and contexts of use. Mobile devices were included in our crossmedia system due to three main reasons: first, their important role as part of these type of ecosystems. Some interesting examples on how mobile devices can enhance the TV experience, in particular, are presented in [5]. Second, the majority of TV consumers watch TV contents in a multi-display environment and the preferred device to serve as a "companion screen" is the smartphone [6]. Third, due to the mobile devices (smartphones) characteristics, which allow the addition of functionalities to enhance mobility and flexibility to an environment. As to our third generation prototype, running from iTV, PC and mobile devices, it provides users with the possibility to choose, from a video, usually watched in a more experiential cognitive mode (which allows us to perceive and react to events naturally), which topics they would want to know more about. They may also choose with which level of detail they want those topics to be addressed, and later decide when and where they would want to access those extra related contents (a web-based content), in a more reflective mode (the mode of thought), and with whom they would want to share them with, having the adequate support from the application in the different access contexts. Important to refer that the mentioned generated web-based extra related content, also referred to as a personalized informal learning content, will be referred along the text, simply, as web content. Also important to refer that the web content is generated by the user, from scratch, and solely based on their choices. After being automatically generated by the user, the web content may be viewed and edited, from any of the devices involved (iTV, PC and mobile devices), and additional videos, pictures, sounds, GPS coordinates, etc, may be easily added to the web content. Nothing in the web content is suggested by default by the system. Considering that the architecture and the main features available in iTV and PC contexts were already explored and described in previous publications [7–10], this paper will focus on the introduction of mobile devices and their specific functionalities and design challenges in this crossmedia video-based environment.

After this introduction, Sect. 2 includes a review of related work and concepts, Sect. 3 describes the design challenges of crossmedia applications and mobile devices in that context, Sect. 4 presents the design decisions on the crossmedia eiTV mobile device module, and Sect. 5 presents the results of the evaluation. Finally, Sect. 6 presents the conclusions and perspectives for future research and developments.

2 Related Work

This section addresses some of the more relevant related research studies with a main focus in Crossmedia environments that include mobile devices. A comparative discussion on these works vs. our application is also presented.

The TAMALLE project [11] developed a 'dual device system' for informal English language learning, based on iTV and mobile phones, supporting learners of English as a second language in their TV viewing, selecting what to access later on the mobile phone. This was an interesting crossmedia system capable to accommodate different cognitive modes and different contexts of use, especially, if considering the mobile phone possibilities. This work was important to our research due to the good results achieved by providing users with mobility in the use of the system thus being able to accommodate different cognitive modes and different contexts of use, especially, if considering the mobile phone possibilities. However, it is more limited in options and scope than eiTV, considering that the only output device was the mobile phone, only used as an output device, and thus functionalities in order to take the best advantage on the mobile phone characteristics were not considered.

Obrist et al. [12] developed a crossmedia "6 key navigation model" and its interface for an electronic program guide running (EPG) on the TV, PC and mobile phone. The different devices were not used in a complementary way since the intention was basically to test a similar interface, on three different devices, which was based solely on six specific keys. They have reached important results since they have perceived what works best and what does not, in particular, that viewers prefer a reduced number of navigation keys and a unified User Interface (UI) with the same functionalities across devices. This study showed that it is important to have a reduced number of navigation keys. However, that does not mean that the interface which requires a lower number of keys will necessarily be the preferred one and the more effective. This indicates that a balanced solution between effectiveness and usability should be found. The authors also state that the concept also shows its advantage in allowing crossmedia usage, namely, the navigation concept use on PCs and mobile devices. The results of this study support our decision of developing UI prototypes adapted to a reduced number of navigation keys. However, and contrary to this work, in eiTV the devices are supposed to work in a complementary way.

Newstream [13] provides extra information about what is being watched and related websites, using TV, PC and mobiles. Depending on the viewers' needs, that extra information may be viewed immediately, stored for later view or pushed to other device. Each device maintains awareness of each other and is able to: move interaction to the device that makes the most sense in a specific context, use several devices simultaneously, and use the mobile device as a remote to the TV and PC. The focus that distinguishes their work from other experiences is the focus on crossmedia content. Limitations, in spite of the technically well designed "ecosystem of devices", are the fact that, the system relies almost exclusively on social networks to: receive and share content and for interaction and dialogues. As to the viewer direct influence on the new contents presented as extra information, is limited. In fact, those contents are presented based on the whole and not particular issues within that story. What distinguishes eiTV from Newstream is the viewers' possibility to choose exactly which issues they are interest in knowing more about, the ability to generate that extra information which may be edited and complemented with the viewers' input (text, images, video, music), the fact that the system does not rely on social networks, in spite of having the possibility to share those extra contents with social networks contacts (if the viewer has them) and is not limited to a single genre, it was already implemented on two different genres: documentaries and film series. As to functionalities, in Newstream they are very different between devices. TV is used to watch videos and the mobile phone interface has five tabs: one that allows using it synchronized as a remote control for TV or PC, and four other tabs entirely focused on the community built around the video, and act independently of the TV interface. This allows viewers to interact with their social network, find new media, and browse different clips, all without affecting the content shown on the TV. As to eiTV, all the devices are prepared with the same basic features in spite of some devices specific features.

2BEON [14] is an iTV application which supports the communication between viewers, textually and in real time, while watching a specific program. It also allows viewers to see which of their contacts are online, which programs they are watching, and instant messaging on the iTV, demonstrated to be important to give viewers a sense of presence. Currently called WeOnTV, it is being implemented with smartphones as "secondary input devices", soon to be distributed by one of the most popular Portuguese TV cable companies. This work demonstrates the importance of sharing information with viewers' contacts about what they are watching on TV, which supports our own decision of including a sharing functionality in eiTV.

Segerståhl [1, 15] proposed the 'Polar Fitness System' a crossmedia fitness support system, which includes a wearable heart rate monitor and an interoperable web service. Along with the heart rate monitor, accessories such as a GPS receiver, a heart rate monitoring strap, and a USB dock for transferring data to the web are included. The wrist unit provides immediate information (during the exercise) on factors such as heart rate, calories, time and distance and tools for planning, monitoring and following-up fitness activities. After each exercise, the wrist unit provides feedback as well as a weekly summary with suggestions for the next week. The web service, that is supposed to be accessed through the PC, includes a training calendar and tools for creating long-term training programs as well as detailed exercise plans, and "information and instructions for heart-rate-based exercise. It also provides progress charts, graphs and summaries for analytic and long-term follow up, a place to document exercising and a long-term storage for exercise data" [15]. In sum, in order to access the complete information, users are supposed to access the web service. The crossmedia fitness system was an interesting contribution but did not achieve all its goals. As it was used, the system even changed the ways in which subjects trained, and in some cases even their main goals. For example, a participant found out how he could use the collected heart rate information in order to regulate his recovery times between weight lifting sets while training, meaning that the wrist unit by itself succeeded. However, the system was not perceived by all users as crossmedia, because the system was not presented as a whole unit. Since the wrist unit interface was not designed in a way that reminded the user that a web service was available, the contextualization failed. This work was an important contribution considering that it helped showing the importance of presenting the system as a whole unit, something that needs to be understood by viewers since the first moment, thus making part of their conceptual image of the system. Another relevant dimension is contextualization which failed in the system and must be assured in order to keep viewers aware of contents amongst transitions.

Nadamoto and Tanaka [16] have developed ways to automatically transform web content into TV-program-type content as a first step towards media fusion. As to the generated TV-program-type content, in spite of being presented in TV style, it may be watched from TV, PC and mobile phones. Their transformation systems are based on creating audio and visual components. In this work they used "text read-out and dialogue techniques for transforming the audio component, and image animation and character agent animation types for the visual component". By combining these techniques, they were able to transform web content into various types of TV program content, which may be fused with various broadcast programs and watched from any device. In sum, they have proposed a 'TV-style presentation' system capable of searching the web, extracting related and relevant web pages, automatically transforming the text and image based web content found into audio-visual TV - program type content - through the use of character animated agents and text read-out; and fusing it with normal broadcasted TV program contents. In technological terms, starting points are TV and web and arrival points are TV, PC and mobile phones. This work addressed the need for extra and complementary content, however that content was transformed in order to be integrated with the information source. The results have shown the usefulness of their approach, and also the need to refine the fusion of transformed web content with TV program content. In fact, the final result became too much intrusive, and, contrary to our application, the authors are not offering a personalized solution prepared to react to changes in viewers' cognitive modes, which may be more passive or active and change in seconds, requiring easily adaptable systems.

The NoTube project [17] is a second screen system. A second screen systems implies the use of TV as main source of information and the simultaneous use of other devices, e.g. smartphones, laptops, tablets, as companion, in order to allow viewers interaction with the TV content. The NoTube uses the web as a useful companion to the TV and had the vision of bringing Web and TV closer together via shared data models and content across multiple devices. The system exploits the richness of data on the Web in order to enhance the TV experience. Social web viewers' activities are analyzed to create continuously evolving user profiles and, based on that the system is able to recommend interesting programs. In this system, TV is not bound to the device: the computer may be used as a TV and vice-versa, while the mobile device may be used as a remote control. The system includes a feature called N-Screen which was designed to help answer the question "What shall we watch?" independently of people location. Imagine a group of friends in different rooms: each one can drag and drop interesting programs to a specific friend in N-screen, or to the whole group, in order to show directly their preferences. When someone receives a new program from a friend in N-Screen, s/he can click on it to see more information about it (basically, it is a drag and drop of movie trailers). Once the N-Screen group has found something interesting to watch together, one of them can drag and drop it to the TV and it will play on the shared TV screen. The system was designed to be used in conjunction with an out-of-band communications channel (e.g. face to face chat, Skype, or IRC) for the direct negotiations. It was initially developed for tablets and laptops but runs on any device with a modern Web browser; from smartphones to tablets and desktop PCs. As to the second screen, it is used to choose and control, and then, when ready, play on a large screen. Concluding, users can share recommendations with friends via multiple personal devices in real time. And with the second screen "TV controls watching together-apart becomes a reality" [17]. Important to mention that the NoTube is, in sum, a recommendation system that allows crossmedia sharing with friends and has several features. N-screen is described here, because it is the closest to our research. In fact, it addresses the social side of TV, the importance and the need of being connected and the importance of sharing contents. Applications should be flexible enough in order to accommodate these functionalities. Through N-screen, viewers find movie trailers of interest which they are able to share with friends in an easy way. However, this share functionality does not include any kind of personalization or adaptation to different cognitive modes, contrary to eiTV. The eiTV application is second screen. Both mobile and PC devices may be used to interact with the TV set: in order to show the same content that is being watched from the TV; show, previously generated, web contents related to what is being watched from the TV and show the video that was used to generate the web content that is being watched from the TV.

In the era of the second screen, the American channel ABC has developed an iPad application, called 'My Generation Sync app for iPad', for its show 'My Generation'. The application, available for download on the web, installs a new app in the iPad. From there, the user may activate the synchronization mode and then freely interact directly with the TV program. The user may vote, answer quizzes and get real time results, comment the TV content, consult detailed information about the characters, go behind the scenes and discover details about the show, etc. It is one of the best applications of its kind and as stated by Guérin [18], the slogan could not be more explicit: "Change the way you watch TV". It was advertised as an innovative application: one screen in your hands, one screen on the wall[1], and brings to TV watching the benefits of a second screen, to free the TV screen of extraneous info, while providing more control to the viewers,

---

[1] More information available at: http://www.youtube.com/watch?v=ZY6oJR38OoI.

as also explored in research projects. In conceptual terms, it is a very well designed, friendly and usable system. It addresses the social side of TV, the importance and the need of being connected and able to interact with the program as well as the need to know more about certain issues. However, the only way to access the system functionalities is through the use of two different devices simultaneously, which is limited in terms of flexibility. In fact, the viewers may change their cognition mode and prefer to see the extra information only through one device. The system could be more flexible to accommodate user preferences allowing both options: the use of a second screen or not, as it happens with our eiTV application.

Livingston [19] proposed the Cronkite system which provides extra information to viewers of broadcast news. Cronkite is the only crossmedia system, referred in this related work section, that does not use mobile devices. However, it was considered important to our work. While viewers are watching a news story, they feel the need to know more about it, they press the "interest" button on their remote and the system provides them with extra information on the computer display. The extra information, with pointers to other related stories, is about the story that they are watching rather than specific topics of interest inside the story, which is somehow limited. To have the system working, both TV and PC need to be simultaneously on. The system is limited considering that the extra information is not stored for latter view (and that might be the viewers' preference). The paper clearly addresses the need of further similar research in this area which was exactly what we did but expanding the functionalities, the devices in use and without the limitations of Cronkites' system. Our application stores the related information for later use and iTV, PC and mobile devices are used, simultaneously, or not. Viewers may select very specific topics of interest inside a story instead of the whole story, and some specific functionalities, as asynchronous communication tools, were also contemplated as well as the inclusion of mobile devices due to their advantages in terms of mobility.

3 Design Challenges

This section describes the central aspects, cognitive and affective, that need to be considered to effectively design crossmedia services and interfaces, with a special focus on the design challenges associated with video and mobile devices.

3.1 Crossmedia Design Challenges

Media and Cognition: Norman's view [20] defines two fundamental cognitive modes. The experiential mode allows us to perceive and react to events naturally and without cognition, but require different technological support, and the medium affects the way we interpret and use the message and its impact on us. For example, TV and video are typically watched in an experiential mode, but learning strongly relies on reflection. A successful integration of media should have into account what each medium and device is most suited for in each context of use, augmenting and complementing their capabilities in a flexible combination.

Crossmedia Interaction, Conceptual Model and User Experience: The main challenges of crossmedia interaction design described by [1] include: consistency, interoperability, and technological literacy needed for the different devices. The conceptual model, how the software will look like and act, is also a very important aspect, since several interaction scenarios and contexts are involved [21]. The quality of the interaction cannot be measured only by the quality of its parts, but as a whole. In this context, the user experience (UX) may be evaluated through how well it supports the synergic use of each medium and the different kinds of affordances involved, also understanding what makes the user pass the current medium boundaries to use other media as well. According to [22], the UX may involve the isolated perception of the medium (distributed), one of the biggest barriers to its efficient use and adoption, or the perception of the system as a whole unity (coherent). According to [23], the UX evaluation methods and measures relevant, when ubiquitous TV is involved, are: physiological data; data mining, log files, observation, case studies, lab experiments, experience sampling method, probes, diaries, interviews, surveys and focus groups. The combination of methods to use depends on each specific case.

Supporting Crossmedia HCI: In this context, the migration of tasks is supported via crossmedia usability and continuity, influencing on how well and smoothly users' skills and experiences are transferred across the different devices [24]. The consistent look and feel across media is an important requirement, even if it should not limit the goal of having each medium doing what it is most suited for and extending its characteristics (synergic use) [25].

Designing for Different Devices and Contexts of Use: Crossmedia design involves designing interfaces for different devices. To understand the devices, and have each device doing what it is most suited for, the best approach is usually to study each particular situation, including device characteristics and cognitive and affective aspects associated to its use: why people use them, in which mode, compare them, etc., and the design guidelines for each device [8] followed by an adequate combination.

3.2 Mobile Devices Design Challenges

Interactive systems design has always been a hard task considering the diversity of factors that were involved and thus requiring the designer's attention, ranging from the final users needs to the context in which the solution is going to be used. More recently, the appearance of mobile and ubiquitous computing supported through different and new devices, and as in our particular case as part of a crossmedia application, contributed to a substantial increase of opportunities and challenges associated with the design process for these new devices.

Due to the specific characteristics of mobile devices, namely, their ubiquitous and permanent nature, small dimensions, several interaction modalities, the multiplicity of possible contexts of use, these devices interfaces are becoming extremely hard to design, but nevertheless very desirable in many contexts, and in particular in our application, due to their flexibility, mobility and location awareness.

As to the main challenges of mobile devices design, they are spread through the design process phases [26]:

1) *Analysis and requirements recoil:* on mobile scenarios where the use of the mobile device or application is constantly based on mutational contexts, where users may be walking and passing through different places and environments, the recoil of requirements is a difficult task and needs a specific approach;
2) *Prototyping:* prototyping techniques that support the construction and evaluation of prototypes in realistic scenarios is needed. In general terms, all components (device prototype and UI prototype) must be as faithful to the original as possible;
3) *Evaluation:* Recent research experiences suggest that given their intensive and pervasive use, mobile devices and correspondent applications should be evaluated on multiple and realistic settings [27]. There are also design guidelines for mobile devices that we took into account. For example, Brewster's [28] set of guidelines to overcome the limited screen space, Kar et al. [29] guidelines about the system's usability, Sánchez et al. [30] navigational hints to the construction of mobile web pages, and Apple [31] guidelines for SmartPhones.

4   Mobile Devices Design in eiTV

This Section presents main functionalities and design options concerning mobile devices in the eiTV Crossmedia system, in response to the challenges identified in Sect. 3.

4.1   Mobile Devices Design Process

As stated by several authors, when designing applications and interfaces to mobile devices, the design and development process should be transported out of the laboratory [26], which was exactly what we did, along with taking into account the design challenges and guidelines addressed in Sect. 3, in addition to traditional design guidelines in User-Centered Design methodologies. The specific mobile device challenges identified in Sect. 3 were addressed as follows:

In the Analysis and Requirements Recoil Phase: It was decided to pay attention to the user behaviour changes according to the surrounding environment, the variables that trigger the changes and how they affect usability. For this, we used the framework proposed by [26] which defines three main modular concepts: conceptual scenarios (scenarios composed by a set of variables as location, persona, device, etc); scenario transitions (used to demonstrate that a change occurred from one contextual scenario to another); and scenario variables (locations and settings; movement and posture; workloads, distractions and activities; devices and usages; users and personas). As to the position or attitude, it is usually a lean forward position that implies an active attitude and a more reflexive cognition mode.

In Prototyping: We separated the physical prototype (the device) and the GUI prototype while building a realistic graphical UI in the high-fidelity prototypes. Real devices (TV, PC and mobile) were used and all the functionalities were implemented in breadth and depth. The *evaluation* is described in Sect. 5.

4.2   Mobile Devices Functionalities

In the mobile devices, the central functionalities of the eiTV system are present: Create, Search, Share and Profile. These functionalities are available: at the 'departure point', which occurs while watching the video and generating the web content, and at the 'arrival point', when accessing/editing/etc. the generated web content. Although these functionalities allow the same actions as on iTV and PCs, they were not provided exactly in the same way, considering the different devices characteristics. To briefly remind these central functionalities: Create allows users to watch videos and select topics of interest to create further information; the Search functionality searches videos based on different criteria and allows to watch them, and edit the associated generated web content if there is one; the Share functionality allows sharing the generated web content, or retrieved video, with user's contacts; and the User Profile contains personal data in order to personalize the generated web contents.

In order to have each device doing what it is most suited for, contexts of use, device characteristics and cognitive and affective aspects associated to its use were studied. In what concerns to *specific mobile devices functionalities,* after this study, the following were made available:

1) *Great flexibility and mobility* (use it everywhere, anytime, anyway): when using the TV, the scroll is not an option, but that does not happen when using the other devices; contrary to TV and PC, mobile devices may be used everywhere, even when users are standing up, mining that any extra time may be used (if waiting for a medical appointment, in a bus queue, while in the train, etc);
2) *Location-based search using the GPS functionality:* the search functionality allows users to search videos related to their current location. As an example, when near the liberty statue the user may use this functionality to search, from its own system and the internet, videos related to that specific spot (this type of video files need to be inserted when using iTV or PC);
3) *Add immediately, or latter, shot pictures or videos,* that may be *related,* to the video being watched, as additional information to the web content or, instead, really integrated as part of the web content.

4.3 Mobile Devices Design Options

As part of a larger crossmedia system, the design challenges identified in Sect. 3 were considered in the mobile devices design module. As to the cognition modes, all functionalities (central or specific to mobile contexts) were designed to accommodate users' changes in cognition modes, attention levels, and different levels of technological literacy or preferences. Namely: they may be more or less intrusive of the video watching experience, designed with 3 different information levels (named in the system as 1, 2 and 3), ranging from less to more intrusive and informational (see Fig. 1b, where the '1; 2; 3' option is available at the bottom of the screen and where you can see that the level 2 is activated), prepared to be viewed immediately or latter, overlaid or embedded onscreen, etc; if viewers turn off the device when in the middle of generating a web content, all the selected topics, will be stored and the web content will be generated; the user has a simplified navigation layout that takes advantage of the typical smartphones navigation characteristics as the scroll bar, tactile screen, etc. Thus, a simplified interface, when compared to the other devices (PC and iTV), was possible. Nevertheless different levels of intrusion were made available; on the search functionality, a specific location may be inserted through text or through the GPS of the mobile device; shot pictures or videos (stored or capture at that time) may be inserted as additional information to a web content at any moment.

Consistency in UX and the perception of the system as a whole coherent unity independently of the device being used was also a priority. In spite of having considered the mobile device characteristics and contexts of use in the design, towards a more simplified design, we decided to keep a coherent layout in terms of colours, symbols and other graphic elements, as navigational buttons, in order to better contextualize users, give them a sense of unity in their UX and to allow a smooth transition among media and devices. This way, it was possible to provide users with a sense of sequence and continuity, respect the context of use and be consistent in terms of look and feel and navigational options in all the devices, and to help the perception of the application as a unity. Users are aware that they may access their eiTV application through different devices whenever they create web contents, helping to conceptually understand the system as an 'ecosystem of devices'. An example of the resulting mobile module design interface is presented in Fig. 1. Considering that it is the main focus of this paper, but not the only one, the presented interactions (Fig. 1) are exclusively from mobile devices. However, this interaction proposal was already developed and tested on the other eiTV devices (iTV and PC), obviously taking into account these devices specific characteristics.

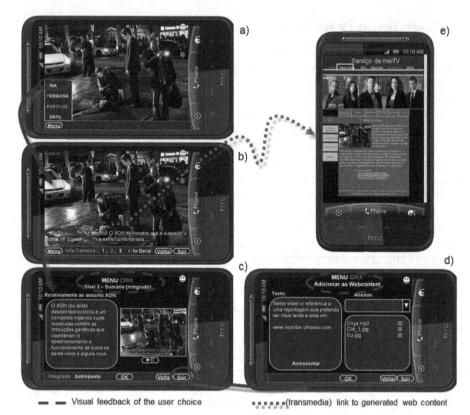

— — Visual feedback of the user choice   ▪▪▪▪▪▪ (transmedia) link to generated web content

Fig. 1. eiTV Mobile Interface *Create* functionality (a); topics selection interface with the information level 2 activated (b); additional information immediately presented when a topic is selected by the user and the information level 2 is activated (c); interface to the addition of files captured on the moment to the web content being created (d); interface of the generated web content, based on the users selected topics (b–e)

5 Evaluation

The UX evaluation methods and measures considered relevant for this specific case as a final evaluation were: observation, case studies, lab experiments, experience sampling method, questionnaires, interviews and focus groups [32].

The evaluation group was composed of 38 participants: 8 experts, that were selected from the HCI and iTV academic research areas, 7 are university teachers, ranging from 34 to 60 years old, 3 female and 5 male, which have collaborated in previous usability evaluation phases (and which feedback is not included in the presented results) and 30 participants, ranging from 18 to 60 years old, which were grouped into 3 evaluation groups, namely:

- group 1: composed of 10 students from the Information Systems Management Degree, ranging from 18 to 34 years old, 5 female and 5 male, with high technological literacy.

Five of them already participated on the previous evaluation and 5 were new (meaning that they participated for the first time);

- group 2: composed of 10 students from the Marketing Degree, ranging from 18 to 30 years old, 5 female and 5 male, with medium technological literacy. Five of them already participated on the previous evaluation and 5 were new;
- group 3: composed of 10 persons from the general public, with a low scholar level ranging from 8th to 12th grades, ranging from 32 to 60 years old, 5 female and 5 male, with low technological literacy. Five of them already participated on previous evaluation and 5 were new.

The decision about using previous and new evaluators in all the literacy groups was based on the assumption that with the experienced ones we would get richer insights about the implemented improvements in terms of interfaces, functionalities, how easy it is to learn how to use the application, etc. These participants were important to maintain a conceptual idea of the whole application and allowing to ask for comparisons. With the new participants, it is possible to perceive the application first impact with all the functionalities already implemented in all the devices.

As to the participants technological literacy categorization, it was possible via the use of a questionnaire with questions as: do you use Internet? e-mail? Facebook? How many hours a day? From which devices? Do you have a smartphone? Which functionalities do you use on your smartphone? etc.

The evaluation process, which was carried out inside the school campus, from June to December 2015, started with a demonstration of the last tested high-fidelity prototype on a PC (this last tested high-fidelity prototype didn't include mobile devices, it only comprised iTV and PC), in order to remind users and to create a sense of unity of the whole application. Then, users were asked to perform tasks that allowed using all the eiTV functionalities (central and also mobile specific ones, already described in Sect. 3), designed for mobile devices, through the prototype in three different contextual scenarios, and devices, with transitions between them. Users started using the prototype, by generating a web content, through iTV at a simulated 'living room' environment at school. The web content was later accessed, and personalized, via PC and mobile (in the same 'living room'). Then, they used the PC to generate a second web content which was later, viewed and personalized via TV and mobile (at the simulated 'living room'). Finally, they used the mobile to generate the third web content while seated at the school bar. Then, they moved to the school backyard, created a video and searched related videos by GPS coordinates (*Location-based search using the GPS functionality*) which were added to the web content in order to personalize it. Then, they entered the school and used the mobile to take a picture, add the metadata manually, and add the picture to the web content. Next, they moved to the bar and, standing up at the end of the bar queue (similar to other public queues), they personalized the web content with their GPS coordinates. Finally, they moved to the library that, although surrounded by people, is a quiet place (context similar to a medical clinic waiting room) in order to view the final web content and use the SEARCH functionality. Note that during the changes of context, the luminosity conditions, as well as the surround conditions (noise), changed when going from the building interior to the exterior, and vice versa. The interaction with the GUI high-fidelity prototype occurred, mainly, via the smartphone but also via

PC and iTV. It is important to mention that the evaluation process took place in real contexts of use, one of the most important factors to consider when testing crossmedia applications.

Finally, viewers were asked to fill a questionnaire and were interviewed. The questionnaire was based on the USE questionnaire (usefulness, satisfaction and ease of use) [33]; the NASA TLX questionnaire (cognitive overload) [34]; and usability heuristics. Results are presented next. At both the 'departure interface' (generate the web content through mobile device), and 'arrival interface' (access that web content) as presented in Tables 1 and 2: The mobile interface was considered easier to learn than the TV and PC interfaces. At the 'departure interface', the TV and PC interfaces were considered more pleasant visually and better designed than the mobile interface. At the 'arrival interface', only the PC interface was considered more pleasant visually and better designed than the mobile interface. Important to note that, when compared with previous results from mixed-fidelity prototypes, these results are good.

Table 1. Evaluation of eiTV overall departure and arrival interfaces

eiTV crossmedia system		Easy to learn	Visually pleasant	Well designed	Could be better
Departure interface	TV	73%	87%	73%	87%
	PC	80%	83%	80%	70%
	Mobile	**93%**	73%	60%	87%
Arrival interface	TV	63%	70%	67%	90%
	PC	87%	87%	80%	67%
	Mobile	**93%**	80%	73%	87%

In terms of information level, more users preferred level 1 (the less intrusive and less informational) on mobile and TV than on PC. This result stresses an increase in users preference to select additional info to access later on when they are watching video on the move with a mobile, when compared with TV or PC, where users already prefer this option not to interrupt the more experiential mode of watching videos.

Table 2. Evaluation of eiTV overall departure interfaces (information levels)

eiTV crossmedia system		Most used information level		
		1	2	3
Departure interface	TV	**47%**	40%	13%
	PC	37%	**43%**	20%
	Mobile	**50%**	33%	17%

In general, the central functionalities Create, Search, Share and Profile (see Tables 3 and 4) were considered more interesting, ease to use and useful, than in previous tests with mixed-fidelity prototypes [35]. As to the most important ones in the context of the application (Create and Search) they were also considered more interesting. As to specific actions inherent to the use of mobile devices: all users appreciated the idea of mobility (100%), the possibility to use GPS in location-based searches (100%), and the possibility to add pictures and videos to the web content, at that particular moment or later, both related and unrelated to the video being watched (100%). Most functionalities were considered more difficult to use, if considering the smaller screen size and font (63%), but easier (87%) if considering the interaction mode (tactile screen versus mouse and remote). These aspects, along with having the access to the web content in the same device that created it, also influenced (decreased) the perceived need for contextualization at arrival.

Table 3. Evaluation of the create and search functionalities from TV, PC and mobile departure interfaces

Characteristics	Create			Search		
	TV	PC	Mobile	TV	PC	Mobile
Interesting	87%	83%	**93%**	73%	70%	**100%**
Ease to use	80%	87%	*67%*	77%	87%	*63%*
Useful	87%	90%	**100%**	87%	80%	**93%**

Table 4. Evaluation of the share and profile functionalities from TV, PC and mobile departure interfaces

Characteristics	Share			Profile		
	TV	PC	Mobile	TV	PC	Mobile
Interesting	77%	87%	*83%*	67%	63%	*60%*
Ease to use	73%	80%	*73%*	47%	73%	**80%**
Useful	77%	83%	**93%**	57%	73%	*70%*

It is important to mention that the intention of transmitting a sense of unity was achieved: 93% of the users referred that they immediately felt "inside" the same application, in spite of using a different device (Table 5).

Table 5. Evaluation of contextualization from departure to arrival interfaces

	Sense unity	Context with video or image need	Context with video playing need
TV	80%	83%	77%
PC	80%	93%	73%
Mobile	**93%**	87%	60%

As a whole, the eiTV crossmedia application with the mobile devices was considered (Table 6): more useful, easy to use, easy to learn, and more users would like to have it and would recommend it to a friend, when compared to having only iTV and PCs, with high percentages.

Table 6. Overall evaluation of the whole eiTV crossmedia application

Whole application	Useful	Easy to use	Easy to learn	Like to have	Recommend
TV & PC	87%	73%	67%	87%	80%
TV & PC & Mobile	**100%**	**77%**	**87%**	**100%**	**100%**

In general, there was no substantial difference of opinion amongst the 3 evaluation groups. Nevertheless, it was possible to observe that the group with poor technological literacy, in general, took more time to accomplish the proposed tasks and asked more questions. However, like the other 2 groups, they all made it and the enthusiasm was the same. Interesting to note, no considerable differences were detected between the group with high technological literacy and the group with medium technological literacy. This may be explained by the fact that half of the participants had already participated on previous eiTV evaluations so they are, probably, more familiar with it.

6 Conclusions and Future Work

The evaluation results were very encouraging. In many aspects, the increased functionalities and flexibility inherent to the mobile context were perceived as useful and an added value in this crossmedia context (e.g., location-based search). Some design options allowed to accommodate the users cognitive mode changes (e.g., information levels), and the prototypes where designed and tested in real mobile scenarios, and contexts of use simulated to look like real ones. In general, the results showed that the integration of the mobile devices in the eiTV application was a success. Considering the design framework followed, the trends in the use of multiple devices, and the results of this and previous studies, we have reasons to believe that our goal for this crossmedia context is worth pursuing and that we can achieve quite good results with all the devices in different scenarios. The results achieved, and the presented conclusions, are in accordance with the research needs identified in the related work presented in Sect. 2 and corroborate the results obtained in other studies. As previously mentioned, the system developed in this work was carried in 2015. The achieved results were an important contribution to research in what concerns to the identification of the design challenges that need to be addressed in crossmedia environments, considering the mobility aspect. After an analysis of the crossmedia systems evolution since 2015, it is possible to say that the identified design challenges remain a valid and relevant contribution to this research area. Also important to mention that these design challenges also helped to identify other challenges that emerged and will be addressed in future work.

As to future work, we intend to explore technological advances (in terms of devices and also in general terms) in order to create new functionalities capable to better support users needs, different cognitive modes and flexibility as for instance a functionality which allows having contents suggested by default by the system, a functionality that allows to interact with the system through voice commands and natural language, etc. A continuous improvement of the interfaces, so that in the future they may become easier to learn and use considering that, as stated by Abreu et al. [36], the future of usability is based on the reduction of the effort of interaction between the user and the system. Another goal is to prepare the system to be adopted by specific groups of people, as for instance, people with visual impairments and older (senior) populations. In what refers to visual impaired viewers, some recent studies proposing new approaches for the creation of audiovisual translation techniques [37], will be considered in order to improve and adapt our eiTV application. In what refers to the senior population and considering that the ageing of the population is an undeniable fact, faced by almost all countries, we also intent to contribute to their inclusion. There are several strategies, supported by governments and researchers, in order to improve senior's quality of live [38]. The use of technology for many purposes, ranging from entertainment to health support, is one of these strategies. However, seniors have difficulties in daily tasks which increase when the tasks involve the use of any type of new technologies, due to the fact that the use of these technologies require a higher cognitive, visual and motor capacity [39]. The only way to overcome this situation is to adopt new design and development strategies [40] which we intend to follow in a near future.

Acknowledgments. This work was partially supported by FCT through LASIGE Multiannual Funding and the ImTV research project (UTA-Est/MAI/0010/2009).

References

1. Segerståhl, K.: Utilization of pervasive IT compromised? Understanding the adoption and use of a cross media system. In: Proceedings of 7TH International Conference on Mobile and Ubiquitous Multimedia (MUM 2008) in cooperation with ACM SIGMOBILE, Umea, Sweden, pp. 168–175 (2008)
2. Jenkins, H.: Transmedia missionaries: Henry Jenkins. http://www.youtube.com/watch?v=bhGBfuyN5gg. Accessed 05 Oct 2019
3. Bates, P.: T-Learning - Final Report. Report prepared for the European Community IST Programme, pjb Associates (2003). http://www.pjb.co.uk/t-learning/contents.htm. Accessed 23 Oct 2019

4. Taplin, J.: Long time coming: has interactive TV finally arrived? Opening keynote. In: Proceedings of 9th European Conference on Interactive TV and Video: Ubiquitous TV (EuroiTV 2011), Lisbon, Portugal, p. 9. ACM (2011)
5. García-Crespo, A., García-Encabo, I., Matheus-Chacin, Carlos A., Diaz, María V.: Mobile devices, a complement to television. case studies. In: Abásolo, M.J., Abreu, J., Almeida, P., Silva, T. (eds.) jAUTI 2017. CCIS, vol. 813, pp. 3–14. Springer, Cham (2018). https://doi.org/10.1007/978-3-319-90170-1_1
6. Fraile, I., Núñez, J., Malewski, S., Artigas, X., Fernandez, S., Llobera, J.: An end-to-end toolset for the creation and delivery of video-based multi-device content. In: Proceedings of JAUTI 2017 – 6th Iberoamerican Conference on Applications and Usability for Interactive TV, Aveiro, Portugal, pp. 154-161 (2017)
7. Prata, A., Guimarães, N., Chambel, T.: Crossmedia personalized learning contexts. In: Proceedings of 21st ACM Conference on Hypertext and Hypermedia (HT 2010), Toronto, Canada, pp. 305–306 (2010)
8. Prata, A., Chambel, T., Guimarães, N.: Personalized content access in interactive TV based crossmedia environments. In: TV Content Analysis: Techniques and Applications, CRC Press, Taylor & Francis Group (2011). ISBN 978-1-43985-560-7
9. Prata, A., Chambel, T.: Going beyond iTV: designing flexible video-based crossmedia interactive services as informal learning contexts. In: Proceedings of 9th European Conference on Interactive TV and Video: Ubiquitous TV, EuroiTV 2011, Lisbon, pp. 65–74 (2011
10. Prata, A., Chambel, T.: Metodologia para avaliação de soluções crossmedia geradoras de ambientes personalizados de aprendizagem informal a partir de vídeo. In: Actas do seminário entre a teoria e o conhecimento – Investigar práticas em contexto, Portugal, Setúbal, 30 October 2014. http://www.si.ips.pt/ese_si/web_gessi_docs.download_file?p_name=F15666 83053/C9.pdf
11. Pemberton, L., Fallahkhair, S.: Design Issues for Dual Device Learning: interactive television and mobile phone. In: Proceedings of 4th World Conference on mLearning - Mobile Technology: The Future of Learn in Your Hands (mLearn 2005), Cape Town, South Africa (2005)
12. Obrist, M., Moser, C., Tscheligi, M., Alliez, D.: Field evaluation of a cross platform 6 key navigation model and a unified user interface design. In: Proceedings of 8th European Interactive TV Conference (EuroiTV 2010), Tampere, Finland, pp. 141–144. ACM (2010)
13. Martin, R., Holtzman, H.: Newstream. a multi-device, cross-medium, and socially aware approach to news content. In: Proceedings of 8th European Interactive TV Conference (EuroiTV 2010), Tampere, Finland, pp. 83–90. ACM (2010)
14. Abreu, J.: Design de Serviços e Interfaces num Contexto de Televisão Interactiva. Doctoral thesis, Aveiro University, Aveiro, Portugal (2007)
15. Segerståhl, K.: Crossmedia systems constructed around human activities: a field study and implications for design. In: Gross, T., Gulliksen, J., Kotzé, P., Oestreicher, L., Palanque, P., Prates, R.O., Winckler, M. (eds.) INTERACT 2009. LNCS, vol. 5727, pp. 354–367. Springer, Heidelberg (2009). https://doi.org/10.1007/978-3-642-03658-3_41
16. Nadamoto, A., Tanaka, K.: Complementing your TV-viewing by web content automatically-transformed into TV-program-type content. In: Proceedings of the ACM Multimedia' 2005, Singapore, pp. 41–50 (2005)
17. Aroyo, L.: NoTube exploits the richness of data on the Web to enhance the TV experience (video file) (2012). Video posted to http://notube.tv/2012/03/26/notube-exploits-richness-of-web-data-to-enhance-tv-experience/

18. Guérin, L.: Transmedia, crossmedia, multimedia, plurimedia... What if we had to describe these notions to someone working in a completely different field? Transmedia Lab (2010). http://www.transmedialab.org/en/economics/transmedia-crossmedia-multimedia-plurim edia-et-si-nous-devions-expliquer-ces-notions-a-quelquun-qui-travaille-dans-un-domaine-dactivite-completement-eloigne-2/

19. Livingston, K., Dredze, M., Hammond, K., Birnbaum, L.: Beyond broadcast. In: Proceedings of ACM IUI 2003, The Seventh International Conference on Intelligent User Interfaces, Miami, USA, pp. 260–262 (2003)

20. Norman, D.: Things that Make Us Smart. Addison Wesley Publishing Company, Reading (1993)

21. Norman, D.: The Design of Everyday Things. Basic Books, New York (2002)

22. Segerståhl, K., Oinas-Kukkonen, H.: Distributed user experience in persuasive technology environments. In: de Kort, Y., IJsselsteijn, W., Midden, C., Eggen, B., Fogg, B.J. (eds.) PERSUASIVE 2007. LNCS, vol. 4744, pp. 80–91. Springer, Heidelberg (2007). https://doi.org/10.1007/978-3-540-77006-0_10

23. Obrist, M., Knoch, H.: How to investigate the quality of user experience for ubiquitous TV?. Tutorial. In: Proceedings of EuroiTV 2011, 9th European Conference on Interactive TV and Video: Ubiquitous TV, Lisbon, Portugal (2011)

24. Florins, M., Vanderdonckt, J.: Graceful degradation of user interfaces as a design method for multiplatform systems. In: Proceedings of the ACM International Conference on Intelligent User Interfaces (IUI 2004), Funchal, Madeira, pp. 140–147 (2004)

25. Nielsen, J.: Coordinating User Interfaces for Consistency. The Morgan Kaufmann Series in Interactive Technologies, San Francisco (1989). Neuauflage 2002 edn.

26. de Sá, M.: Tools and techniques for mobile interaction design. Doctoral thesis, Lisbon University, Lisbon, Portugal (2009)

27. Nielsen, C., Overgaard, M., Pedersen, M., Stage, J., Stenild, S.: It's worth the hassle! The added value of evaluating the usability of mobile systems in the field. In: Proceedings of 4th Nordic Conference on Human-Computer Interaction (NordiCHI 2006), Oslo, Norway, pp. 272–280 (2006)

28. Brewster, S.: Overcoming the lack of screen space on mobile computers. Pers. Ubiquit. Comput. 6, 188–205 (2002)

29. Kar, E., Maitland, C., Montalvo, U., Bouwman, H.: Design guidelines for mobile information and entertainment services – based on the Radio538 ringtunes i-mode service case study. In: Proceedings of 5th International Conference on Electronic Commerce (ICEC 2003), Pennsylvania, USA, pp. 413–421. ACM Press (2003)

30. Sánchez, J., Starostenko, O., Castillo, E., González, M.: Generation of usable interfaces for mobile devices. In: Proceedings of CLICH 2005, pp. 348 (2005)

31. APPLE: iOS Human Interface Guidelines. http://developer.apple.com/library/ios/documenta tion/userexperience/conceptual/mobilehig/MobileHIG.pdf. Accessed 08 Feb 2020

32. Prata, A., Chambel, T.: Mobility in a Crossmedia environment capable of generating personalized informal learning contents from iTV, PC and mobile devices. In: Proceedings of JAUTI 2019 – VIII Conferência Iberoamericana sobre Aplicações e Usabilidade da TV Interativa, Rio de Janeiro, Brasil, pp. 59–71 (2019)

33. Lund, A.: Measuring Usability with the USE Questionnaire. http://www.stcsig.org/usability/newsletter/0110_measuring_with_use.html. Accessed 23 Oct 2011

34. NASA: NASA TLX – Paper/Pencil Versin. http://humansystems.arc.nasa.gov/groups/TLX/paperpencil.html. Accessed 23 Oct 2011

35. Prata, A., Chambel, T.: Mobility in a personalized and flexible video based transmedia environment. In: Proceedings of UBICOMM 2011, Fifth International Conference on Mobile Ubiquitous Computing, Systems, Services and Technologies, Lisbon Portugal, pp. 314–320 (2011)

36. Abreu, J., Santos, R., Silva, T., Marques, T., Cardoso, B.: Towards proactivity behaviours in voice assistants for the TV ecosystem. In Proceedings of JAUTI 2019 - VIII Conferência Iberoamericana sobre Aplicações e Usabilidade da TV Interativa, Rio de Janeiro, Brasil, pp. 165–173 (2019)
37. Oliveira, R., Abreu, J., Almeida, M.: Involving visually impaired viewers in the design of accessible solutions for audiovisual translation. In: Proceedings of JAUTI 2017 – 6th Iberoamerican Conference on Applications and Usability for Interactive TV, Aveiro, Portugal, pp. 34-46 (2017)
38. Silva, T., Reis, L., Hernández, C., Caravau, H.: Building informative audio-visual content automatically: a process to define the key aspects. In: Proceedings of JAUTI 2017 - 6th Iberoamerican Conference on Applications and Usability for Interactive TV, Aveiro, Portugal, pp. 130-141 (2017)
39. Johnson, J., Finn, K.: Designing User Interfaces for an Aging Population (2017). https://www.uxmatters.com/mt/archives/2017/04/designing-user-interfaces-for-an-aging-population.php. Accessed 23 Jan 2019
40. Pinho, A.: Estudo de User Experience de uma interface tangível: O cubo personalizável SIX, Master thesis, The University of Aveiro, Portugal, 6 December 2019

Interaction Techniques and Technologies

Training Natural Language Understanding for the TV Context: A Visual Stimuli Approach for the Elicitation Process

Rita Santos[1]([✉]) [ID], Jorge Ferraz de Abreu[2] [ID], Pedro Almeida[2] [ID], Pedro Beça[2] [ID], and Tiffany Marques[2] [ID]

[1] DigiMedia, Águeda School of Technology and Management, University of Aveiro, 3754-909 Aveiro, Portugal
rita.santos@ua.pt

[2] DigiMedia, Department of Communication and Art, University of Aveiro, 3810-193 Aveiro, Portugal
{jfa,almeida,pedrobeca,tiffanymarques}@ua.pt

Abstract. Voice User Interfaces (VUI) are giving promising steps towards interaction scenarios based on natural language interpretation rather than simple voice commands. The adaptation of these systems for each usage context requires a deep training process of the Natural Language Understanding component with the support of human collaboration.

Among the several phases involved in the training process, the first step, aimed at gathering a significant number of distinct "natural" phrases/expressions for each action to be addressed by the system, needs to be tackled very carefully.

To be successful in collecting a significant number of phrases related to the intents to be made active in the system, it is important to stimulate participants in a way that promotes diversity on the uttered phrases. This task demands a methodology that allows participants to be triggered in an abstract way, avoiding them to be directly influenced by the stimulus presented to them.

This paper reports on different stimulation strategies to prompt participants (either in group or individually) to utter distinctive phrases associated with natural language interaction with a TV set. The elicitation process that was designed was supported by visual stimuli which included still frames of video content and TV system user interfaces (showing content or apps), pictograms, comics and movies. Results show that, in general, the use of this kind of techniques can originate a significative number of diversified and relevant phrases specially if the user is familiar with the content used in the strategies.

Keywords: Voice User Interfaces · Natural language interaction · Television · Taxonomy · Visual stimulus · Pictures

1 Introduction

Voice User Interfaces (VUI), integrated in TV consumption scenarios, are paving the way towards supporting the interaction on natural language rather than simple voice

© Springer Nature Switzerland AG 2020
M. J. Abásolo et al. (Eds.): jAUTI 2019, CCIS 1202, pp. 89–102, 2020.
https://doi.org/10.1007/978-3-030-56574-9_6

commands. However, reaching this goal requires a deep training process of the Natural Language Understanding (NLU) component with the support of human collaboration.

During an interaction by natural language, the user can adopt a wide set of words and expressions to reach a certain goal, implying that the NLU responds correctly to a wide linguistic diversity of possible words and phrases sustaining the interpretation of the users' real intentions. This is especially relevant because for someone interacting with a VUI, saying something like "I'm in the mood for watching a funny movie" or "Show me a movie that makes me laugh" (or any other similar phrase), should be interpreted by the system as a simple intent like "search for comedy movies". However, when interacting with participants collaborating in the training phase it is important to avoid confining their answers with the presented stimulus to gather the aimed diversity of words and phrases. With this aim, pictures (drawings, photographs, icons, etc.) have been pointed as a particularly valuable visual stimuli to generate spontaneous phrases, with more variability [1–3].

However, one topic that seems to have been out of discussion is the use of visual stimuli with different characteristics and the suitability of these representations for the elicitation process. This paper reports on elicitation methods based on different types of pictures that were used to collect data to populate and train the NLU component of a natural language processing (NLP) system for a TV broadcaster's set-top box (STB), operating in Portuguese. With the results here presented, it is intended to contribute to survey visual stimuli for phrase collection for such systems and to better understand which can be better suited to provide training data for particular actions related with the television lexicon.

After this introductory section, this paper is structured as follows: Sect. 2 presents information concerning NLU component and strategies based on visual stimuli to collect data to populate and train it, while Sect. 3 presents the adopted methodology. Section 4 presents the experiments. Results, discussion, and conclusions and future work are presented on Sect. 5.

2   The Use of Visual Stimuli for NLU Training

The NLU is the NLP component that deals with the complex challenge of responding to inputs that do not follow well-defined rules, converting them into a structured form that the remaining system understands, being able to respond to - that is, it refers to the reading and understanding of words and phrases in order to extract intents in the application domain [4, 5]. The main reason for this complexity is that people can express an intention in a wide variety of ways [6, 7].

Training is a fundamental step for the good performance of a natural interaction language voice system. In this process, it is important to consider the domain and lexicon for which the NLP service is being developed, not forgetting that the more variance of utterances the better the NLP will be trained [8]. Furthermore, in order to train system models based on machine learning, large amounts of data need to be collected [9].

In order to increase the amount of data for training the NLU, researchers are turning to crowdsourcing approaches which present advantages as expedition, individuality of people, and low cost [9, 10]. While presenting these benefits, one of the challenges about this type of approach is how to ensure naturalness and variety of gathered data [1]. To accomplish this, researchers have been using and evaluating several elicitation techniques as the use of pictures which presents the great advantage of not biasing people by putting words into their mouths [10]. In some contexts, visual stimuli have already proved to be capable of generating more spontaneous and natural utterances, with more variability [1]. However, previous research highlighted that pictures, when compared with textual stimuli, tend to introduce more noise and to omit information that is important to be in the utterance as well as to be more demanding in terms of production [3]. In this framework, one aspect not found in the reviewed studies was the use of different types of visual stimuli (cartoons, single drawings, picture stories, photographs, ...) and the different results that they can generate.

3   Study Design

This study aimed to contribute to the NLU training process of an interactive TV (iTV) system in a Portuguese context, with the goal of developing a fully functional system with a natural language interaction. Taken this in consideration, different visual stimuli related with the users' actions in the iTV context were produced to be used in three data collection stages, before going on to a more advanced training phase at participants' houses. This section begins by presenting the domains and intents considered on the overall process and an overview of the visual stimuli used to collect data to populate and train the NLU component, ending with the general description of the data gathering process.

3.1   Domains and Intents

The first step on our research was to identify a set of domains and intents related with the television context. These were selected taking into consideration that voice interaction is perceived to be more likely used when complex instructions are at stake, that require a significant number of steps for its completion, being cognitive demanding (involving a high number of clicks on the remote control). Furthermore, the most frequent actions related with an iTV STB were also considered. Based on these criteria, the domains and intents considered as priority were:

– **Channels selection** - change to a specific channel by name.
– **TV content search** - search a content by name/title; search content by thematic; search channels by thematic; search trending TV content.
– **Automatic TV-recordings** - access to past contents of a TV channel.
– **Navigation** - access to TV STB menus; access to the EPG (TV Guide) of a channel; get information about the TV content; continue watching; advance to next episode.
– **Video Store** - see contents of a certain type (recent, highlights).
– **TV-apps** - search TV-apps by type; Open TV-apps by its name or when asking for specific information.
– **YouTube** - search content; search content of a pre-existent category (recent videos, more popular, etc.).

3.2 Visual Stimuli Used for Data Gathering

A set of stimuli with different graphic characteristics was developed throughout the study, resulting in different types of representations, some more realistic, others using a more symbolic language, and others more directed to telling a story. Hence, for the purpose of this research the following visual stimuli (and their potential advantages) were considered (Fig. 1) (during the study, some variations of some of these stimuli were created).

1) **Frames of video content** - only the video content is presented, with no other information as the logo of the TV channel.
2) **Frames of the user interface of the iTV STB (contents or apps)** - real images that are thus easily recognized.
3) **Pictograms** - representations of TV content using icons, simplified drawings, with a high level of abstraction.
4) **Comics** - able to introduce a context to the participants, in an abstract way, by its storytelling nature and
5) **Short movies** - video content showing the interaction of a user with the TV in specific situations.

3.3 Data Gathering Process

The gathering sessions took place in three phases. The first phase took the form of a *vox populi* (vox pop) performed individually and in groups, and the next two phases (phase

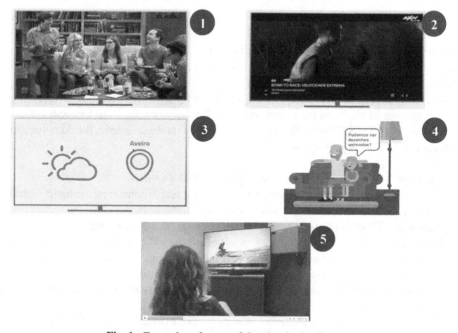

Fig. 1. Examples of some of the visual stimuli used

two and three) were supported by group sessions of two to three people in a laboratory simulation of the interaction with the system via a TV remote with a microphone. The planning of the various phases as well as the development of the visual stimuli and the dynamization of the data gathering sessions were always carried in a formative perspective, with the outputs of the previous phases being considered for the design of the following phases.

4   Experimental Procedures and Results

In this section, the experimental procedures and corresponding results of the three gathering phases are presented.

4.1   Phase One: Vox Pop

For the vox pop approach different visual stimuli were used according to the domains and intents one wished to train. For example, frames of video content were used for the collection of popular TV shows, while pictograms were used for the collection of phrases to train the intent related with content search by thematic. To prevent the user from forgetting that he was interacting with the TV, a dialogue balloon with the word "television" was presented together with the visual stimulus (Fig. 2).

Fig. 2. Examples of visual stimulus presented in the vox pop approach

Three sessions were held between July and August 2018, 2 sessions in group (one group of 2 individuals and another of 3 individuals) and 1 session individually. The sample included adults, teenagers, and children.

4.1.1   Experimental Procedure

Each session consisted of 30 tasks related to 4 of the domains and intents previously established (search a content by name/title, search content by thematic, Open TV-apps saying its name or when asking for some content, search content of a pre-existent category on YouTube), which used video-frames of films and series (10), pictograms (12), TV system frames with app content (4), and comics (4).

At the beginning of each session, participants were informed that the objective was, in addition to gathering phrases for training a voice interaction system using natural language, to analyze various methodologies to collect phrases with different visual stimuli.

The tasks (grouped according to the different visual stimuli) were shown on a tablet and for each task participants were asked to verbalize at least one sentence (although they could utter more than one). When pleased with their performance, the participant(s) could move on to the next task. The person promoting the vox pop had the role of introducing the task, giving the necessary explanations at the beginning of each task and instigating a brainstorm without influencing the sentences generated by the participants.

4.1.2   Results and Discussion

In total, 205 phrases were collected (only two were duplicated) from the 30 prepared tasks, with the individual session generating 29 sentences and the two groups' sessions generating a total of 176 sentences (an average of 35 sentences per participant). Pictograms generated 77 sentences, films and series video-frames generated 50 sentences, followed by comic chat (25) and TV system frames with app content (24). Considering the average number of phrases per task instigated by each stimulus (considering that the number of tasks with each stimulus varied) we can conclude that the collected number of phrases was higher in pictograms, having observed that this stimulus allowed a higher level of abstraction, followed by comic chats, and lastly by the video-frames. Within the frames, the number of phrases was slightly lower when presenting only video content (movies and series) than with TV-apps frames (Fig. 3).

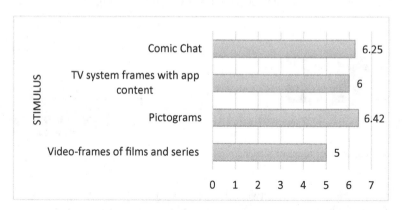

Fig. 3. The average number of phrases per task for each stimulus

Although allowing a good performance when comparing with other stimuli, the Comic Chat task took more time to be explained and raised great doubts in the participants. Therefore, it will not be the best option if the collection procedure was to be extended to a larger number of participants. For these reasons, it was decided to exclude this visual stimulus on the following phases.

In the group approach, the participants sometimes said more than one sentence for each task, which did not happen in the individual sessions. However, since all people can potentially speak at the same time in a group, it happened that sometimes participants, instead of saying complete sentences, simply made changes in the sentences of other participants or, when interrupted, left the sentences incomplete. One way to overcome this problem can be using a mediation device allowing participants to share complete, isolated, and independent sentences. Another issue to improve is related to the way the tasks were presented. At this stage, the tasks were presented on a tablet, but it would have been a better option to show the images on a larger screen, such as a monitor or a TV.

4.2 Phase Two: Simulated Lab Interaction with the System via a TV Remote with a Microphone

To allow a broader coverage of the various domains and their related intents, presented in 3.1, and based on the information gathered in the previous phase, another set of sessions was carried out.

Three sets of tasks (A, B and C) were defined, each including 15 tasks. The intents referring to the tasks are presented in Table 1. The tasks were relatively similar between the groups. As an example, Task 1 (which intent was "search content by thematic") involved asking for action movies in set A, asking for musicals in B and asking for romantic movies in C.

Table 1. Information about the tasks considered in phase two

Task	Intent	Stimulus[*]
1	Search content by thematic	1, 2
2		1, 2
3	Open TV-app saying its name or when asking for some content	1, 2
4		1, 2
5	Search TV-apps of a certain category	1
6	Open the EPG of a TV channel	1, 2
7	Access to contents of the previous days of a TV channel	1
8	Search a content by name	1, 3
9	Access to TV STB Menus	1
10		1
11	Ask for a trending content	1, 3
12	Search channels by thematic	1, 2
13	See contents of a certain type on the Video store	1
14	Search content of a pre-existent category	1, 2
15	Change to a specific channel	1, 2

[*] 1- frame of the iTV system user interface; 2- pictogram; 3 – video content frame

For each task of each set (A, B, C), a representation based on frames of the iTV system user interface was used. Furthermore, for some of the tasks, an alternative version (using pictograms or video content frames) was created when it was considered that it would be a reliable option (see Table 1). In this way, 6 groups of tasks were prepared to be presented to the participants: A1, A2, B1, B2, C1 and C2.

Figure 4 presents an example of Task 6 variants in group A: open the EPG of the History Channel. Considering the close to reality simulation, the dialogue balloons considered in the phase 1 were removed in this stage, because they were not considered relevant to understand the images and their goal.

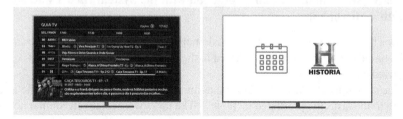

Fig. 4. Examples of stimulus presented in task 6 for A1 (left) and A2 (right)

The sessions were carried out with groups of 2 to 3 people in a lab context in the Aveiro University facilities. Participants, mostly academics (students, scholarship holders and researchers), were settled in 18 small groups (16 with 2 participants and 2 with 3 participants), and each group performed one group of tasks. In the end, each group of tasks (A1, A2, B1, B2, C1 and C2) was repeated 3 times. In total, 38 participants took part in the study, with ages raging from 17 to 46 years old, 55.3% were male and 44.7% female. Of the 38 participants, 89.5% reported having a Pay-TV service.

4.2.1 Experimental Procedure

The sessions followed five steps: **1**- Welcoming the participants with the offer of a snack and a drink; **2** - Presentation and contextualization about the study; **3** - Explanation of the general procedure - stimulated by the images presented in a monitor, the participants were asked to use a TV remote control with an integrated microphone, to record their sentences. Although the system was unable to react to the participants' requests, this pseudo-interaction approach aimed to provide a more realistic scenario than the one used in phase one. It also helped to reduce the level of noise and the number of overlapped phrases. Participants were told that: the dialogue with the TV should be as natural as possible and that they could discuss ideas with each other; the phrases should start with "Television … "; there were no right or wrong answers and that creativity was valued; **4** - Completion of tasks (each session consisted of a set of 15 images and participants should say "next" to move to the next image); **5** - Fill in a characterization questionnaire. The researcher supervising the test session was responsible for registering the participants' opinions on what they considered to be important in an ILN context, which domains/intents they would most often use and other participants' observations or failures during the test.

The contextualization of the study, the explanation of the procedure and the presentation of the tasks were carried with the support of a multimedia presentation that also included demonstration videos.

4.2.2 Results and Discussion

In total, 1882 sentences (49.52 sentences per participant) were collected, of which 1862 were unique. The TV system frames allowed to collect 1289 sentences, stimuli based on pictograms allowed to collect 456 sentences and video frames 137 sentences. When considering the average number of phrases per task instigated by each stimulus (considering that the number of tasks with each stimulus varied), it is concluded that the collected number of phrases was higher in video frames (68.5), followed by TV frames (64.5), and lastly by the pictograms (57).

The total sentences collected within A1, B1 and C1 sets of tasks (with only TV video frames) was 1003 and in the case of A2, B2 and C2 (where alternative stimuli were used for some tasks) was 879. The number of sentences generated for the different intents is presented in Fig. 5.

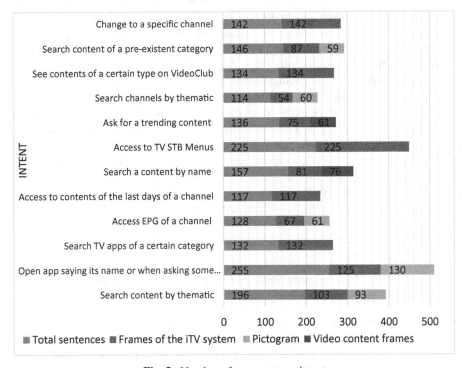

Fig. 5. Number of sentences per intent

Task 8 generated the higher number of sentences (157), with the stimuli represented by TV system frames (81 sentences) showing better results than the stimuli with video frames (76 sentences). The stimulus based on TV system frames that generated more sentences (89) was presented on task 15 and the stimulus based on pictograms that generated more sentences (69) was presented on task 3 (Fig. 6).

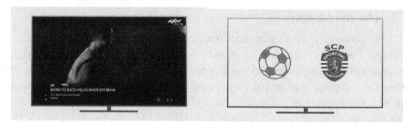

Fig. 6. TV system frame in task 15 (left) and pictogram in task 3 (right) that generated more sentences

The stimuli generating more sentences evoked interest and/or personal knowledge of the content presented (Football, YouTube, movies). In turn, stimuli that generated fewer sentences were referred to as topics that were unknown or uninteresting to participants.

Comparing the performance in the tasks where different stimuli were used, it was possible to conclude that in some cases pictograms performed better than TV system frames but in others the opposite happened. However, it was possible to conclude that TV system frames allowed to collect a higher number of sentences, being clear that the abstraction inherent to the pictograms sometimes limited the participants' reaction. After the first participant saying a sentence, the other (or remaining) felt that the right answer was already said (Pictionary game-like effect) and usually was unable to generate more sentences. However, this "Pictionary effect" did not happen when participants had a deep knowledge of the shown pictograms (e.g. a football club logo generates a large number of sentences, a "baby" pictogram generates sentences about movies and children channels). On the contrary, the TV system frames offered more visual affordances. Even though the most obvious words in the interface were said in the first sentence, there were usually other words or images that other participants could use to generate sentences. This may also justify the fact that in tasks where video content frames were used as an alternative to TV system frames the former had a worse performance.

4.3 Phase Three: Focus Group Sessions to Survey Phrases Related to Three Specific Domains/Intents

During the training of the voice system, it was considered important by the partner of the project (AlticeLabs, the research branch of Altice, the company that owns the bigger IPTV platform in Portugal) to gather phrases related with three quite challenging domain/intents: "Trends" (popular TV-shows), "Continue watching" (continuing to see a content/movie that had been interrupted) and "Next episode" (asking for the following episode of a TV-series when one ends).

Following the process of exploring visual stimuli methodologies to collect phrases with semantics relevant to the television context, new stimuli were created: hybrid TV frames with a small pictogram with the name of the content included and motion pictures with recorded sound. The first was used to obtain sentences related with "Trends" (Fig. 7). Based on a preliminary survey of the Portuguese television trend contents for 2019, as well as on everyday trends, 10 images were created for each of the following categories:

Entertainment/Lifestyle, Sports, Movies, Series, and Information. Videos were used to obtain sentences associated related with "Continue watching" and "Next episode".

Fig. 7. Example of stimulus used to collect sentences related with Trending content

Regarding the intents "Continue watching" and "Next episode", two videos were created:

- Continue to watch a movie that went halfway[1] - the video shows a person falling asleep while watching a movie and, later, shows the user holding a remote control and navigating through the application in order to continue watching the movie;

- See next episode on Binge Watching[2] - the video shows a person watching a series and, when the episode ends, it is presented the user taking the remote control and navigating to next episode.

In this phase, another set of sessions was carried at AlticeLabs premises. The sample consisted of 29 participants, ranging in age from 16 to 48 years old, 3 female and 26 male. 14 groups were formed, with each group corresponding to one test session. Of these 14 groups, 13 were composed of 2 participants and 1 of 3 participants.

4.3.1 Experimental Procedure

This phase followed similar steps as the previous one:

1. Welcoming of the participants followed by a brief characterization.
2. Presentation and contextualization of the study.
3. Explanation of the general procedure, namely, how to proceed to record the sentences using the remote control.
4. Completion of tasks – each group, instead of being assigned with the same tasks, was given the option of choosing a thematic (or more than one), from the Trending

---

[1] Video available at https://youtu.be/v-ey6tE4cDw.

[2] Video available at https://youtu.be/bpYyZGBiHaI.

topics that participants felt most comfortable with. Participants were asked to utter a sentence that could be used to ask, in a creative way, to the television/STB for the content or action presented in the representations. Also, participants could make requests related to what they saw. Participants were also asked to utter sentences related with the intents "Continue watching" and "Next episode".

4.3.2 Results and Discussion

Regarding the set of trending contents chosen by the participants, sports was the most chosen thematic (7 times), TV-series was the second one (6 times), followed by information and movies (5 times each), and last entertainment (4 times). Continue watching and next episode were selected 11 times each. In this phase, a total of 1063 sentences were collected. These can be grouped in: trends (244), next episode (48), continue watching (40) and meta information (731) – this implies to know specific characteristics related to the TV trends (for example, in what position is Sporting (a Portuguese football team) in the European league or who is playing against Sporting).

Regarding the phrases used for requesting trending contents, participants provided a higher number of sentences in the TV-series category (76), followed by sports (49) and movies (42). The categories least requested and which resulted in a lower number of sentences were entertainment/lifestyle (39) and information (38). The average number of phrases per task in each category (considering that the categories were not chosen at the same number), was higher in the TV-series theme, followed by entertainment/lifestyle, information and lastly by movies and sports (Fig. 8).

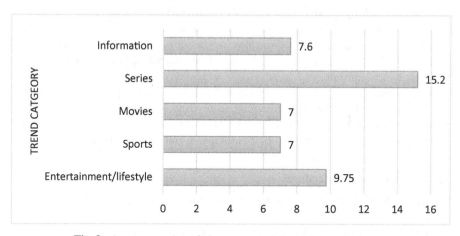

Fig. 8. Average number of phrases per task for each trend category

With only 11 duplicated phrases, it was realized that this data collection approach allowed participants to provide varied sentences regardless of the categories chosen.

During the study, it was observed that the option to split by thematic made participants to feel more motivated as they are doing the tasks with stimuli of their interest. In what regards the motion pictures visual stimuli, it was verified that it makes the experience lighter and more enjoyable. It takes longer to prepare but have in fact proved to be the best option when it is intended to show a context for the action that is inherent to the intent.

5 Conclusions

The study had an exploratory nature in what regards the domains and intents and the visual stimuli-based methodologies. Nevertheless, the collection procedures carried in this study generated important insights for future similar activities. First, we can say that the simulated interaction environment revealed to be a more dynamic way to generate reactions from participants when compared with vox pop. In addition, visual stimuli can often be adopted as a representation that allows to communicate in a clear and unambiguous way the context in which the user is expected to interact, and additionally to represent scenarios sufficiently open to generate great diversity of unique phrases (our study showed that the number of repeated sentences in the different phases was very small). Considering the visual stimuli, pictograms showed to be less efficient when participants did not have a deep knowledge about the subject that the stimuli represented - although, in other cases, their higher level of abstraction allowed them to perform better than other stimuli in some situations. In cases where is important to provide some context, movie pictures revealed to be a suitable option, but comics did not reveal to be efficient. Frames of video content (where only the video content is presented) revealed, in general, to be one of the most efficient stimuli. Also, for this stimulus, it was clear that one fundamental aspect is to guarantee that the participant is familiar with the content, which allows not only the utterance of more valid sentences but also more creative ones. Creativity was also enhanced when performing the tasks in group. One issue that emerged from this research was the fact that there was a significative number of sentences related with the need to know more about the shown content, which highlights the importance of having metainformation and develop a system prepared to respond to that type of requests in order to fulfil the expectations of the users.

It should be emphasized that the phases here presented were carried out with small groups to identify broad aspects, being part of a general process of optimization of a methodology. The points discussed are therefore not intended to represent a sample, but rather to gather a set of assumptions that ultimately aim at improving the training process, and which include all the means, from the analysis of training methodologies to the simultaneous identification of general traits and specifications, that must be taken into account.

As future research, it is planned to apply these visual stimuli in the context of an app that will allow its users to capture sentences in an environment outside the laboratory and without the need of support by the research team. This study will continue with a more advanced training phase at participants' houses of the NLU component of a NLP system for a TV broadcaster's STB, operating in Portuguese.

References

1. Nokinova, J., Lemon, O., Rieser, V.: Crowd-sourcing NLG data: pictures elicit better data. In: Proceedings of the 9th International Natural Language Generation Conference, pp. 265–273. Association for Computational Linguistics, Edinburgh, UK (2016)
2. Braunger, P., Maier, W., Wessling, J., Werner, S.: Natural language input for in-car spoken dialog systems: how natural is natural? In: Proceedings of the 18th Annual Special Interest Group on Discourse and Dialogue (SIGDIAL), pp. 137–146. Association for Computational Linguistics, Saarbrücken, Germany (2017)
3. Dušek, O., Novikoya, J., Rieser, V.: Evaluating the state-of-the-art of end-to-end natural language generation: the E2E NLG challenge. Comput. Speech Lang. **59**, 123–156 (2020)
4. Lola.: NLP vs. NLU: what's the difference?. https://medium.com/@lola.com/nlp-vs-nlu-whats-the-difference-d91c06780992. Accessed 3 Oct 2019
5. Schnelle-Walka, D., Radomski, S., Milde, B., Biemann, C., Mühlhäuser, M.: NLU vs. dialog management: to whom am I speaking? In: Proceedings of the 5th IUI Workshop on Interacting with Smart Objects, p. 4. Sonoma, CA, USA (2016)
6. Benesty, J., Sondhi, M.M., Huang, Y.A. (eds.): Springer Handbook of Speech Processing. SH. Springer, Heidelberg (2008). https://doi.org/10.1007/978-3-540-49127-9
7. Braun, D., Mendez, A. H., Matthes, F., Langen, M.: Evaluating natural language understanding services for conversational question answering systems. In: Proceedings of the 18th Annual Special Interest Group on Discourse and Dialogue (SIGDIAL), pp. 174–185. Association for Computational Linguistics, Saarbrücken, Germany (2017)
8. Singh, B.R.: Chat Bots – designing intents and entities for your NLP models. https://medium.com/@brijrajsingh/chat-bots-designing-intents-and-entities-for-your-nlp-models-35c385b7730d. Accessed 3 Oct 2019
9. Manuvinakurike, R., Paetzel, M., DeVault, D.: Reducing the cost of dialogue system training and evaluation with online, crowd-sourced dialogue data collection. In: Proceedings of the 19th Workshop on the Semantics and Pragmatics of Dialogue (SemDial), pp. 9 (2015)
10. Braunger, P., Maier, W., Wessling, J., Schmidt, M.: Towards an automatic assessment of crowdsourced data for NLU. In: Proceedings of the 11th International Conference on Language Resources and Evaluation (LREC), pp. 2002–2008. European Languages Resources Association (ELRA), Miyazaki, Japan (2018)

Proactivity: The Next Step in Voice Assistants for the TV Ecosystem

Jorge Ferraz de Abreu[1]([⊠]) [iD], Rita Santos[2] [iD], Telmo Silva[1] [iD], Tiffany Marques[1] [iD],
and Bernardo Cardoso[3] [iD]

[1] Digimedia, Department of Communication and Art, University of Aveiro,
3810-193 Aveiro, Portugal
{jfa,tsilva,tiffanymarques}@ua.pt

[2] DigiMedia, Águeda School of Technology and Management, University of Aveiro, 3754-909
Aveiro, Portugal
rita.santos@ua.pt

[3] Altice Labs, R. Engenheiro José Ferreira Pinto Basto, 3810-106 Aveiro, Portugal
bernardo@telecom.pt

Abstract. Intelligent Personal Assistants (IPAs) are increasingly present in people's daily lives, with natural language interaction allowed by voice assistants improving the user experience. In the television ecosystem, the integration of voice assistants is also enabling the interaction with media devices in a globally more satisfying way. Additionally, the inclusion of proactive behaviours is considered to be one of the critical factors for the improvement of the user experience. To better understand this dimension of voice assistants, the present article analyses the proactivity concept and examples of voice assistants that incorporate proactive behaviours. Also, voice assistants have been analysed in the television ecosystem and it was realized a lack of systems presenting a real proactive behaviour able to assist users in a television context.

Keywords: Intelligent Personal Assistants · Natural Language Interaction · Proactive behaviour · Interactive television

1 Introduction

Usability is led by the aim of reducing the user-system interaction effort, with the ultimate goal of having an interface that requires zero cost of interaction [1]. One of the solutions for reducing the effort of user interaction is based on Intelligent Personal Assistants (IPAs), which not only help with daily tasks but also reduce the number of interactions with the device at stake when searching for information.

Interactions with these assistants tend to be conducted in a question and answer format, task oriented [2]. However, the inclusion of artificial intelligence supported by Big Data in IPAs has contributed to a change in how these systems perform tasks and search for information, and how users buy products, interact with businesses, and consume content [3]. These technological advances have also enabled IPAs to evolve from reactive to proactive agents, able to act in advance, making autonomous decisions

© Springer Nature Switzerland AG 2020
M. J. Abásolo et al. (Eds.): jAUTI 2019, CCIS 1202, pp. 103–116, 2020.
https://doi.org/10.1007/978-3-030-56574-9_7

(without user intervention) relevant to the user needs [4] (for example, proactively giving information about traffic and weather conditions before the user leaves home), with the promise of increasing user productivity [5].

Since IPAs have had significant penetration in several devices, especially voice assistants, the scenario of integrating a proactive voice assistant into the actual TV ecosystem (social and technological media landscape associated with both audio-visual and TV fields [6]) seems to be interesting given its potential to add value to the user experience and reduce the interaction effort.

In this context, this paper aims to provide a survey on the concept of proactivity and examples of voice assistants that incorporate this kind of behaviours, as well as analysing the application of this concept on TV IPAs, to inform the design of a proactive voice assistant suited to the TV ecosystem. After this introductory section, the article is structured as follows: Sect. 2 presents the features and challenges of an IPA; proactivity in voice assistants is covered in Sect. 3; Sect. 4 presents the state of proactivity in a television context and some insights on future research in this topic; and final considerations are presented in Sect. 5.

2   A Characterization of Intelligent Personal Assistants

IPAs are software agents that assist users in their daily tasks by presenting information (relevant and personalized) in an intelligent way [7]. They are designed to be personal, knowing who the user is, what he/she does, what are his/her interests and what, when and where he/she needs assistance [5]. Through more dynamic interactions and derivation of unscheduled responses [8], IPAs allow users to reduce their cognitive load [7]. This is possible because they use a range of technologies such as automatic speech recognition (ASR), natural language understanding (NLP), text-to-speech (TTS) synthesis, dialogue management, data mining, analytics, inference and personalization [5]. In addition, IPAs may use machine learning to provide proactive recommendations from contextual data [8]. Recommendations are used to facilitate selection and support decision-making when users are faced with large amounts of information, such as when choosing products or restaurants [9]. In some cases, the paradigm of IPAs seeks to develop Just In Time (JITIR) information retrieval to offer proactive experiences, with the objective of recommending correct information at the right time and thus assisting the user prior to any request [10, 11].

2.1   Features

IPAs facilitate the management of daily tasks, such as booking hotel rooms, shopping and scheduling meetings [12]. To make this possible, IPAs combine various features:

Context-Awareness - The context consists of information about the user's circumstances, which includes information about his/her external environments (e.g.: time and place) and detected user activity (e.g.: devices used, places visited, times and day of the week), gattered, for instance, by mobile devices [10]. It may influence in decision-making when requesting services [13] and/or content. Contextual information, which combines the physical and virtual world, allows a deep understanding of the user. Without this type of information, consultations can be ambiguous and have the potential to be interpreted differently. Context is necessary for a proper interpretation of queries [5].

Integration - One of the tasks of an IPA is to reach and manage other devices. As such, integration with other technologies is crucial. This integration allows the user to access collected measurements, daily tasks and stored information from anywhere. One of the key benefits of integration is improving the context-awareness of a device [14].

Adaptability - IPAs can be trained and make use of machine learning to complete tasks using initial or learned knowledge. Learning ability is essential for a system to be autonomous and adaptable as it allows an IPA to perform behaviours based on its experience [15]. It can deliver better results as it adapts [14] and as it is customized to the user. Personalization allows tuning the availability of content, products and services relevant to the user and answer to their interests, characteristics and needs [16].

Anthropomorphism - In terms of IPAs, anthropomorphism is "a conscious mechanism wherein people infer that a non-human entity has human-like characteristics and warrants human-like treatment" [17, p. 2854]. Luger and Sellen [18] suggest that this feature increases users' expectations of such interactions. Studies have validated that anthropomorphic IPAs provide more efficient communication [19]. However, their degree of anthropomorphism may vary depending on the interface provided to the user [20]. To make human-assisted interaction richer and more natural, the agent's empathy plays a fundamental role [21]. There is evidence that users are more satisfied with an empathic virtual agent [22], considering it more reliable and attentive [23].

Multimodality - Ability to obtain inputs and/or provide outputs in more than one way [18], providing the user with various modes of interaction (vocal, textual, graphic,...). The voice interaction mode has greater weight in the IPAs market compared to other modes of interaction (graphical, textual), being the IPAs that use this way of interaction named voice assistants. Voice interaction is used at both input and output phases, reducing the effort of human-computer interaction. Users can interact not only with voice commands but also using a conversational style [24], depending on the IPA used. A study conducted by [25] found that 72% of users of digital assistants use voice search.

In addition to the features highlighted above, there are other dimensions that can be used to characterise an IPA, such as autonomy (works without human intervention, autonomously delivering information to the user), reactivity (only reacts to clear requests for user information) and proactivity (predicts unmet needs of users) [14]. The concept of proactivity will be discussed in more detail since it is the focus of this paper.

2.2 User Interactions with IPAs

Nowadays, the majority of users make use of IPAs to perform tasks such as showing the weather and searching for information and music [26]. User difficulties when using IPAs, lack of knowledge about IPAs features and the false expectations created about their capabilities and characteristics [27], might cause distrust in the user for the execution of more complex tasks, such as writing emails or making a phone call. In these situations, there is a concern that the IPA might not execute the requested task correctly [18]. Studies [2, 18] indicate that users often have difficulty in understanding how to interact with IPAs, giving the user a sense of overload or resulting in various interactions when trying to test the abilities of IPA. However, the authors of the study [2] also point to a possible connection between user satisfaction and the frequency of use of the IPAs. User satisfaction is also influenced by usability. Kiseleva et al. [28] indicated a negative correlation between user satisfaction and the complexity and effort to complete a task. In addition, the absence of feedback from the assistant on the completion of a task was also pointed out as a reason for user dissatisfaction [18].

In view of the expansion and diffusion of IPAs, there is a clear need to consider contextual social issues (public nature of the context) and the information issued from interactions [29, 30]. A study [30] showed that users prefer to use their IPAs in private locations, even to transmit non-sensitive information. They also avoid voice interaction in public places because of privacy concerns and because it might be socially unacceptable. Social concerns are a significant barrier to the increased use of IPAs by infrequent users of this type of technology [2].

2.3 Challenges

When talking about IPAs, there are some associated challenges. In this section we discuss privacy and security and natural language processing (NLP).

Privacy and Security - When IoT and cloud services are managed by IPAs, the problems associated with these technologies might be reflected in those devices. The IoT devices share to the cloud user data, being such data vulnerable to be used in various fields such as advertising and marketing, raising concerns about privacy [14]. Although IPA is not always recording, it still listens to the user to be able to execute commands [31] or hear wake-up words. This can raise concerns about wiretapping, which is, logically, perceived as a threat to user privacy.

NLP - It is easy for humans to understand language, but this is a rather complex task for machines. Since a term can have different classes (noun, adjective, verb) and meanings, there is still a huge effort to define words. NLP techniques themselves have been insufficient to give meaning to words. However, Big Data has provided breakthroughs in this area, using sequences of speech excerpts to analyse words [32]. Additionally, another of the recognized challenges is the evolution and emergence of new words. Machine training and learning may be insufficient for NLP due to this challenge [33]. Developing IPAs requires progress in the areas of speech recognition, speech analysis, common sense-based reasoning, conversation support, conversation context awareness, simulation of human speech and human gestures and movement [34]. The NLP challenge is a key issue to the authors of this paper since this study is currently focused on the idealization of a proactive IPA for the TV ecosystem, whose main mode of interaction is the voice. Accordingly, the examples discussed in Subsect. 3.2 and Sect. 4 will be of voice assistants.

3   Proactivity in Voice Assistants

Unlike reactive behaviour IPAs, that only respond to clear users' requests, IPAs that present proactive behaviours predict users' unmet needs by analysing their context, preference patterns and behaviours, and automatically provide personalized content [35] without the user's request. The proactive approach thus uses contextual user information to make relevant recommendations when confronted with an appropriate situation [13]. However, it also presumes the analysis of user behaviour and subsequent data synthesis [36]. The data can come from browsing history, purchase history, click behaviours, search patterns [16], location and biometric signs. Proactive assistance uses inference, user modelling and classification to enhance experiences [5].

3.1   Proactive Behaviours: Types and Principles

The user's trust in an IPA is directly related to its ability to perform autonomous tasks aligned with their needs [37]. Both awareness and understanding of (semi) autonomous behaviour are crucial to building trust with the system. An IPA can highlight two types of proactive behaviours: **1) task-focused proactivity:** provides assistance for a task that is already being performed by the user or is already planned; **2) utility-focused proactivity:** assists the user generally with a set of tasks and not with a specific current task [5, 38].

The relevance of the proactive behaviours on an IPA depends on the value they add to the user experience. An IPA is only helping the user if it considers his focus and short and long-term needs. According to Sarikaya and Yorke-Smith et al. [5, 38], to guide the development of proactive behaviours in IPAs, nine principles that reflect the user-centred experience should be considered: **1) Competent** - within the knowledge and skills for which the IPA has been programmed and trained; **2) Unobtrusive** - does not interfere with the attention or activities performed by the user without being requested; **3) Transparent** - intelligible to the user; **4) Safe** - reduces the negative consequences, in the opinion of the user; **5) Anticipatory** - able to understand the opportunities and short and long term needs of the user; **6) Valuable** - provides information according to the user's interests, needs and tasks; **7) Pertinent** - Vigilant regarding the environment and current situation; **8) Controllable** - exposed to analysis with user control; **9) Deferent** - gracefully unimposing. IPAs with proactive behaviours should also learn and continuously adjust the outputs given through the analysis of user contextual information [5].

3.2   Proactivity Levels

The current state of technologies has facilitated the development of devices that help users complete tasks more efficiently, even allowing them to determine how and when to proactively help users [39]. When interacting with IPAs, the user's intention may be explicit, in which the user makes a request for the system to execute an action (reactive behaviour), as can be deduced, in which the assistant sends notifications or suggestions [5] after a context analysis (proactive behaviour). There must be a balance between system and user proactivity because, while users have the information needed to know what tasks to perform, assistants use limited information (contextual) to infer what the user wants [39]. Isbell and Pierce [39] created a continuum of Interface-Proactivity (IP) which expresses the combination of possible actions between user-system to perform a specific task, demonstrating the possible proactivity balances between the two, through proactivity levels (Fig. 1). The continuum is composed of five levels: i) "Do it yourself" - without the assistant's help; ii) "Tells you to pay attention" - outputs (sound, graphic, textual...) for the user to pay attention to some activity/task; iii) "Tells you what to pay attention to" - the assistant sends notifications/alerts; iv) "Makes suggestions" - the assistant gives suggestions to the user; v) "Makes decisions" - the assistant has full autonomy in decisions/task execution [5, 39, 40]. While at level 1 (far left of the continuum) the user is the only responsible for the execution of an action, at level 5 (far right of the continuum) the system has full autonomy in the execution of tasks and decision-making [39].

Interface-Proactivity (IP) Continuum

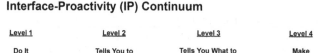

Fig. 1. IP continuum retrieved from [39]

According to this model, the level of proactivity of an interface can depend on a variety of factors, such as user preferences, the context of system use, and confidence in predicting a relevant and appropriate action. Increased confidence allows for a higher level of proactivity. The proactivity of a system has costs/benefits for the user (benefits when the system acts correctly and costs when it performs it incorrectly). At level 1 there are no costs or benefits, since the user is solely responsible for the action. At level 5, there might be significant benefits but also high costs. At this level, the cost of failure can be so high that the user will not trust the system and therefore will not use it anymore. The costs/benefits depend not only on the level of proactivity but also on the application context and situation [39]. In this sense, user expectations may vary throughout the IP continuum [40].

3.3 Examples of Proactive Voice Assistants

Most of the services available today allow search and browse with reactive behaviours, however, several systems with proactive behaviours such as Google Assistant and Microsoft Cortana [41] have emerged in the market. Increasingly, voice assistants with proactive behaviours are being used in a variety of contexts, including home, personal, education, health, and business. From the literature review, examples of commercial and academic voice assistants which use voice as the main mode of interaction were selected:

Google Assistant offers proactive suggestions and personalized information to help the user keep track of everyday tasks, given the context (time and location) and recent interactions with the assistant. The assistant can send notifications such as flight delay alerts, reminders of where the user parked his/her car, personalized music and podcast recommendations, and notifications of nearby activity [42].

Google Maps, like Google Assistant, already shows proactive behaviours in its driving mode feature. Using location history and recent web searches, Google Maps predicts the user's destination and sends notifications about traffic conditions, accidents, and road works [43]. In addition to notifications, Google Maps offers faster alternative route proposals if traffic conditions are not favourable or have changed.

Microsoft Cortana can proactively manage the user's calendar, for example, if it is 8 pm and the user's boss sent an email to arrange an urgent meeting for the following day at 7 am, Cortana will alert the user that an appointment has been made that needs his attention and that he should set the alarm and change his morning routine for the next day [44]. Cortana's proactivity is also reflected in its autonomous creation of content lists (out of five categories: books, film and TV, recipes, restaurants, and shopping) based on Microsoft Edge searches made by the user [45].

Erica is a proactive voice assistant for Bank of America's users, which offers banking assistance to users. It analyses the user's financial data and offers real-time proactive advice for managing and optimizing their expenses, such as suggesting that they reduce credit card usage and/or pay a debt [46].

LISSA provides proactive assistance in the context of students' individual learning process. The assistant programs and monitors the activities that need to be performed by each student, such as lectures and activities related to exam preparation. LISSA adapts to the student's habits and activities, supports their needs, skills and speed of learning, and allows voice interaction. LISSA acts proactively by recommending study materials so that the student can prepare after receiving a notice of the next exam. It proactively sends notifications about changes in the student's academic course. It also automatically records the student's presence at the different academic events, through the location [47].

4 Proactivity in Voice Assistants for the TV Ecosystem

Voice assistants have had significant penetration in several areas and there are already some examples of their integration on the television ecosystem. Systems such as LG Voice Mate (Fig. 2), Google Assistant (Fig. 3), Xfinity (Fig. 4), Alexa (Fig. 5) and Bixby allow to search for TV content without the need to use a remote since the user can interact by voice with the TV. From the analysed voice assistants, two different behaviours related to searching can be observed. For example, when the user says "Quentin Tarantino": **i)** the voice assistants display all content from amongst the various content sources such as YouTube videos and content stored on the television containing that word in the title; **ii)** the voice assistant, after searching the content available on the Set-Top Box and app's, shows movies directed by Quentin Tarantino and other content related to the director.

Regarding proactivity behaviours integration, it was noticed that, so far, in the television ecosystem, these voice assistants do not show proactive behaviours, only present reactive behaviours. A glimpse of proactive behaviours for the home context (including TV interaction) was only identified in the promotional video of the smart speaker Sherpa. According to the manufacturer's, Sherpa uses predictive and proactive AI technology

Fig. 2. LG Voice Mate search results (Retrieved from: https://www.lg.com/hk_en/support/product-help/CT20136005-143505 6283308-others, last accessed 2020/4/17).

Fig. 3. Google Assistant on Android TV – search results (Retrieved from: https://assist ant.google.com/platforms/tv/, last accessed 2020/4/17).

Fig. 4. Context-aware Xfinity VUI for soccer results (Retrieved from: https://www.youtube. com/watch?v=i_PtDTfweAw, last accessed 2020/4/17).

Fig. 5. Activated Alexa on Amazon Fire Cube (Retrieved from: https://www.theverge.com/ 2018/6/21/17484412/amazon-fire-tv-cube-rev iew-alexa-echo, last accessed 2020/4/17).

to anticipate the needs of its users, as in the following example: the user returns from a trip and asks Sherpa what is happening on TV, the latter proactively suggests a comedy content after a tiring trip, however it also provides an action content as an alternative option. Sherpa's solution presents itself as a device connected to the assistant and not as an assistant incorporated in the TV. In addition, it provides only one mode of interaction (voice) [48]. However, it is not clear whether all the reported features of this solution are already on the market.

4.1 Comparison of the Proactivity Levels of Voice Assistants

In view of the examples of commercial and academic solutions mentioned in Subsect. 3.3 and TV solutions presented in this section, a comparative table of these IPAs support regarding the proactivity levels of continuum IP addressed above is presented below (Table 1).

All IPAs show reactive behaviours, positioning themselves at level 1. Regarding proactive behaviour, the analysed IPAs focus their proactivity on level 3 ("Tells you what to pay attention to") and 4 ("Makes suggestions"). Of these IPAs, only three show autonomous behaviour and make decisions (level 5). They autonomously perform activities that, in our opinion, do not have a high failure cost. There is only one (Sherpa), which seems to show proactive behaviours when recommending TV content, being at level 4.

Table 1. Comparative table of IPAs proactivity levels

	Do it yourself	Tells you to pay attention	Tells you what to pay attention to	Makes suggestions	Makes decisions
Google Assistant	Search for information	-	Notification of flight delay alerts; Reminder of where the user parked the car; Notifications of nearby activities	Personalized music and podcast recommendations	-
Google Maps	Search for a location	-	Notification on traffic conditions, accidents and road works	Suggestions for alternative quicker routes	Set the user's destination
Microsoft Cortana	See marked events on the agenda	-	Meeting notifications	-	Autonomous creation of content lists
Erica	See the balance of the bank account	-	-	Suggestions for managing and optimizing expenses	-
LISSA	See subject for examination	-	Notifications of changes in academic course	Recommendations for study materials	Automatically records student attendance at events
LG Voice Mate	Search for comedy films	-	-	-	-
Google Assistant from TV	Youtube search	-	-	-	-
Xfinity	Series search	-	-	-	-
Alexa	Search by film	-	-	-	-
Bixby	Search for TV shows	-	-	-	-
Sherpa Smart Home	Search for action films	-	-	TV content recommendations	-

4.2   Towards a Proactive System for the TV Ecosystem

In this framework there is a window of opportunity for the implementation of a proactive voice assistant supporting an advanced way of interaction with the TV ecosystem. The next steps of this research will be the design and development of a set of prototypes allowing to mirror possible proactive behaviours in a voice assistant for the television context in several domestic situations. It is intended to use contextual information (time, place, biometric data and user activities) from various devices such as fitness wristbands, smartphones, TVs and desktops. The use of Natural Language Interaction (NLI) is foreseen as the main modality of interaction, since it enhances a more natural and human interaction.

A first step will be to analyse the most interesting proactive situations for the television ecosystem, such as:

a. automatically detecting that the viewer may have fallen asleep and on the next user interaction ask if he/she wants to continue seeing the TV program. In this use case, the viewer's biometric signals play an important role as a context source;
b. automatically detecting that a new viewer is in front of the TV and suggesting a new TV show. This could, for instance, help to avoid small children to be faced with adults' content being watched by their parents;

These scenarios will be discussed in focus groups, in order to anticipate the users' receptivity to an assistant with this type of behaviour for TV and to gather important contributions to assist the design and development phases such as to identify the modalities of interaction which, in addition to voice, will be implemented in such prototypes, namely text and/or graphic, and to better identify the challenges, difficulties, advantages and disadvantages of voice assistants with proactive behaviours for the TV ecosystem. It seems important to analyse, for example, how the system should interrupt the content visualization to provide proactive information and how privacy concern issues could be diminished. The results of the focus groups will provide inputs on the next stages of developing a voice assistant for TV.

5   Final Considerations

Despite the great evolution of voice assistants and associated technologies (e.g. artificial intelligence, machine learning,…), there are still few systems with proactive behaviours. Voice assistants exhibit mainly reactive behaviours, mainly searching for specific content requested by the user and its related content.

To design a voice assistant there are some features that should be taken into consideration: the environment and circumstances in which the user is in (context-awareness), the integration with other devices/systems (integration), the ability to adapt as it interacts and learns with the user (adaptability), presenting characteristics similar to humans (anthropomorphism), and the possibility of various forms of interaction (multimodality). Along with these features, proactivity is touted as an asset because it allows for the displaying of content without user requests, taking initiative, predicting user requests and positively contributing to his/her overall experience.

Proactive assistants should be anticipatory in understanding future needs of the user, valuable and relevant in providing relevant information according to the interests of the user and without interfering with the attention or activities performed by the user - unless there is an explicit request from the user. They must be competent within the knowledge and context for which they have been programmed and trained, transparent about what they know about the user, safe, unimposing and controllable by the user. They should also learn and continuously adjust the outputs given, through the analysis of contextual information from the user. These features may raise some concerns to users about their security and privacy, since for the assistant to be proactive it must be constantly listening to be able to anticipate and predict the user' needs.

Through the analysis of the examples of voice assistants mentioned throughout the paper, it was observed that these assistants, in general, are only prepared to proactively send notifications and suggestions. Few assistants are prepared to make decisions on their own. In the television context, most assistants only show reactive behaviour.

The authors are now fully committed to create a proactive voice assistant for the television ecosystem, centred on users' needs which will provide proactive suggestions/recommendations in this context (TV). During this process, we aim to consider also some questions regarding the use of these assistants by specific audiences (e.g. elderly) and also to find out if the proactive behaviours have the potential to improve the "empathy" of the system.

References

1. Budiu, R., Laubheimer, P.: Intelligent assistants have poor usability: a user study of Alexa, Google Assistant, and Siri. https://www.nngroup.com/articles/intelligent-assistant-usability/. Accessed 26 July 2019
2. Cowan, B.R., et al.: What can i help you with?: infrequent users' experiences of intelligent personal assistants. In: Proceeding of the 19th International Conference on Human- Computer Interaction with Mobile Devices and Services (MobileHCI 2017). pp. 1–12. Association for Computing Machinery, New York (2017)
3. McLean, G., Osei-Frimpong, K.: Hey Alexa… examine the variables influencing the use of artificial intelligent in-home voice assistants. Comput. Hum. Behav. **99**, 28–37 (2019)
4. Schweitzer, N., Gollnhofer, J.F., Bellis, E.: Innovation: role of technology in innovation: exploring the potential of proactive AI-enabled technologies. In: AMA Summer Educators' Conference Proceedings 29, pp. IN18–IN19. Blackwell Publishing (2018)
5. Sarikaya, R.: The technology behind personal digital assistants: an overview of the system architecture and key components. IEEE Signal Process. Mag. **34**(1), 67–81 (2017)
6. Abreu, J., Almeida, P., Velhinho, A., Enrickson, V.: Returning to the TV Screen: the Potential of Content Unification in iTV. Managing Screen Time in an Online Society, 1st edn. IGI Global (2019)
7. Maes, P.: Agents that reduce work and information overload. Commun. ACM **37**(7), 30–40 (1994)
8. Earley Information Science.: making intelligent virtual assistants a reality. https://info.earley.com/hubfs/EIS_Assets/EIS-White-Paper-Intelligent-Virtual-Assistant-Reality.pdf. Accessed 25 July 2019

9. Bader, R., Karitnig, A., Woerndl, W., Leitner, G.: Explanations in proactive recommender systems in automative scenarios. In: Ricci, F., Semeraro, G., Gemmis, M., Lops, P., Masthoff, J., Grasso, F., Ham, J. (eds.) First International Workshop on Decision Making and Recommendation Acceptance Issues in Recommender Systems (DEMRA 2011), pp. 11–18 (2011)

10. Sun, Y., Yuan, N.J., Wang, Y., Xie, X., McDonald, K., Zhang, R.: Contextual intent tracking for personal assistants. In: Proceedings of the 22nd ACM SIGKDD International Conference on Knowledge Discovery and Data Mining – KDD 2016, pp. 273–282. ACM Press, New York (2016)

11. Bahrainian, S.A., Crestani, F.: Towards the next generation of personal assistants: systems that know when you forget. In: Proceedings of the ACM SIGIR International Conference on Theory of Information Retrieval (ICTIR 2017). pp. 169–176. Association for Computing Machinery, New York (2017)

12. Santos, J.F.: Intelligent personal assistants solutions in ubiquitous environments in the context of internet of things. Master's thesis, University of Beira Interior (2013)

13. Singh, R., Bedi, P.: Parallel proactive cross domain context aware recommender system. J. Intell. Fuzzy Syst. **34**(3), 1521–1533 (2018)

14. Balcı, E.: Overview of intelligent personal assistants. Acta Infologica **3**(1), 22–33 (2019)

15. Czibula, G., Guran, A., Czibula, I.G., Cojocar, G. S.: IPA – an intelligent personal assistant agent for task performance support. In: IEEE 5th International Conference on Intelligent Computer Communication and Processing, Cluj-Napoca, Romania, pp. 31–34. IEEE (2009)

16. Xiao, B., Benbasat, I.: E-commerce product recommendation agents: use, characteristics, and impact. MIS Q. **31**(1), 137–209 (2007)

17. Purington, A., Taft, J.G., Sannon, S., Bazarova, N.N., Taylor, S.H.: "Alexa is my new BFF": social roles, user satisfaction, and personification of the Amazon Echo. In: Proceeding of the 2017 CHI Conference Extended Abstracts on Human Factors in Computing Systems (CHI EA 2017), pp. 2853–2859. ACM Press, New York (2017)

18. Luger, E., Sellen, A.: Like having a really bad PA: the gulf between user expectation and experience of conversational agents. In: Proceedings of the 2016 CHI Conference on Human Factors in Computing Systems (CHIC 2016), pp. 5286–5297. Association for Computing Machinery, New York (2016)

19. Kim, Y., Sundar, S.S.: Anthropomorphism of computers: is it mindful or mindless? Comput. Hum. Behav. **28**(1), 241–250 (2012)

20. Knote, R., Janson, A., Eigenbrod, L., Söllner, M.: The what and how of smart personal assistants: principles and application domains for IS research. In: Multikonferenz Wirtschaftsinformatik (MKWI), Lüneburg, Germany, pp. 1083–1094 (2018)

21. Hosseinpanah, A., Krämer, N.C., Straßmann, C.: Empathy for everyone? The effect of age when evaluating a virtual agent. In Proceedings of the 6th International Conference on Human-Agent Interaction (HAI 2018), pp. 184–190. Association for Computing Machinery, New York (2018)

22. Prendinger, H., Mori, J., Ishizuka, M.: Using human physiology to evaluate subtle expressivity of a virtual quizmaster in a mathematical game. Int. J. Hum Comput Stud. **62**(2), 231–245 (2005)

23. Brave, S., Nass, C., Hutchinson, K.: Computers that care: investigating the effects of orientation of emotion exhibited by an embodied computer agent. Int. J. Hum Comput Stud. **62**(2), 161–178 (2005)

24. Kiseleva, J., Williams, K., Awadallah, A.H., Crook, A.C., Zitouni, I., Anas-tasakos, T.: Predicting user satisfactions with intelligent assistants. In: Proceedings of the 39th International ACM SIGIR Conference on Research and Development in Information Retrieval – SIGIR 2016, pp. 45–54. ACM Press, New York (2016)

25. Olson, C., Kemery, K.: Voice report: from answers to action: customer adoption of voice technology and digital assistants (2019)
26. Silva, A.B., et al.: Intelligent personal assistants: a systematic literature review. Expert Syst. Appl. **147**, 113193 (2020)
27. Lopatovska, I., Griffin, A.L., Gallagher, K., Ballingall, C., Rock, C., Velazquez, M.: User recommendations for intelligent personal assistants. J. Librarianship Inf. Sci. **52**, 577–591 (2019)
28. Kiseleva, J., et al.: Understanding user satisfaction with intelligent assistants. In: Proceedings of the 2016 ACM on Conference on Human Information Interaction and Retrieval (CHIIR 16), pp. 121–130. Association for Computing Machinery, New York (2016)
29. Easwara Moorthy, A., Vu, K.-P.L.: Voice activated personal assistant: acceptability of use in the public space. In: Yamamoto, S. (ed.) HCI 2014. LNCS, vol. 8522, pp. 324–334. Springer, Cham (2014). https://doi.org/10.1007/978-3-319-07863-2_32
30. Moorthy, A.E., Vu, K.L.: Privacy concerns for use of voice activated personal assistant in the public space. Int. J. Hum.-Comput. Interact. **31**(4), 307–335 (2015)
31. Chung, H., Iorga, M., Voas, J., Lee, S.: Alexa, can I trust you? Computer **50**(9), 100–104 (2017)
32. Hirschberg, J., Manning, C.D.: Advances in natural language processing. Science **349**(6245), 261–266 (2015)
33. Goldberg, Y.: Neural Network Methods for Natural Language Processing. Morgan & Claypool Publishers, Toronto (2017)
34. Kugurakova, V., Talanov, M., Manakhov, N., Ivanov, D.: Anthropomorphic artificial social agent with simulated emotions and its implementation. Procedia Comput. Sci. **71**(1), 112–118 (2015)
35. Zhang, B., Sundar, S.S.: Proactive vs. reactive personalization: can customization of privacy enhance user experience? Int. J. Hum.-Comput. Stud. **128**(1), 86–99 (2019)
36. Chen, T.W., Sundar, S.S.: This app would like to use your current location to better serve you. In: Proceeding of the 2018 CHI Conference on Human Factors in Computing Systems – CHI 2018, pp. 1–13. ACM Press, New York (2018)
37. Duong, T., Phung, D., Bui, H., Venkatesh, S.: Efficient duration and hierarchical modelling for human activity recognition. Artif. Intell. **173**(7–8), 830–856 (2009)
38. Yorke-Smith, N., Saadati, S., Myers, K.L., Morley, D.N.: The design of a proactive personal agent for task management. Int. J. Artif. Intell. Tools **21**(1), 30 (2012)
39. Isbell, C.., Pierce, J.S.: An IP continuum for adaptive interface design. In Proceedings of HCI International (2005)
40. Meurisch, C., Ionescu, M.D., Schmidt, B., Mühlhäuser, M.: Reference model of next-generation digital personal assistant: integrating proactive behavior. In: Proceedings of the 2017 ACM International Joint Conference on Pervasive and Ubiquitous Computing and Proceedings of the 2017 ACM International Symposium on Wearable Computers (UbiComp 2017), pp. 149–152. Association for Computing Machinery, New York (2017)
41. Shokouhi, M., Guo, Q.: From queries to cards: re-ranking proactive card recommendations based on reactive search history. In: Proceedings of the 38th International ACM SIGIR Conference on Research and Development in Information Retrieval - SIGIR 2015, pp. 695–704. ACM Press, New York (2015)
42. Binay, D.: Stay on top of your day with proactive help from your assistant. https://www.blog.google/products/assistant/stay-top-your-day-proactive-help-your-assistant/, last accessed 2019/7/25
43. Toombs, C.: Maps v.9.19 introduces new "driving mode" with traffic updates and ETAs, audio toggle for navigation, and timeline settings. https://www.androidpolice.com/2016/01/12/maps-v9-19-introduces-new-driving-mode-with-traffic-updates-and-etas-audio-toggle-for-navigation-and-timeline-settings-apk-download-teardown/. Accessed Feb 2019

44. Ash, M.: Cortana gets better at helping you manage your busy schedule. https://blogs. windows.com/windowsexperience/2016/01/25/cortana-gets-better-at-helping-you-manage-your-busy-schedule/#78jRfADI2UkWPHJH.97. Accessed 25 July 2019
45. Sarkar, D.: Announcing Windows 10 insider preview build 17017 for PC. https://blogs.win dows.com/windowsexperience/2017/10/13/announcing-windows-10-insider-preview-build-17017-pc/#1mX7dqrZc3VFYqfc.97. Accessed 9 Sept 2019
46. Makadia, M.: Voice assistants and conversational AI – the future of banking. https://www.business2community.com/business-innovation/voice-assistants-and-conver sational-ai-the-future-of-banking-02051355. Accessed 25 July 2019
47. Todorov, J., Stoyanov, S., Valkanov, V., Daskalov, B., Popchev, I.: Learning intelligent system for student assistance – LISSA. In: Proceedings of the 2016 IEEE 8th International Conference on Intelligent Systems (IS), pp. 753–757 (2016)
48. Sherpa AI.: Un Día Con Sherpa Home. https://youtu.be/6DNaffYyDQ8. Accessed 17 Mar 2020

Accessibility

Implementation of a Brain Computer Interface System to Allow TV Remote Control for People with Physical Disabilities

Cristhian Pachacama[1](✉) and Diego Villamarín[1,2](✉)

[1] Universidad de las Fuerzas Armadas – ESPE, Sangolquí, Ecuador
{cjpachacama,dfvillamarin}@espe.edu.ec,
df.villamarin@alumnos.upm.es
[2] Universidad Politécnica de Madrid, Madrid, Spain

Abstract. This paper presents a remote control implementation that allows the control of TV main functions by people with some motor disability in their upper extremities because they aren't able to take the TV control with their hands, thus collaborating with inclusion and digital accessibility. To get this purpose, a Brain Computer Interface BCI helmet was used, its allows the brain-machine interaction using non-invasive electroencephalography signals without causing health problems. An appropriate methodology was designed by cognitive signals with head movements and expressive signals with some face expressions focused on changing channels, volume up or down, turn on/off the TV. To achieve the integration between the BCI helmet and TV, a graphical interface was made on Processing Development Environment, it can recognize the signals generated by the helmet and, with an Arduino controller emits signals with the functions for any TV remote control. For the evaluation tests, we had a group of different ages people to know gestures or movements complexity and usability satisfaction, the results that we've obtain permit us to propose like future works to get a better operation to use more TV remote control functions, for example, to access the menu or participate in interactive TV applications.

Keywords: Brain Computer Interface · Electroencephalogram signals · Motor disability · Inclusive television

1 Introduction

The concept of Brain-Computer Interface (BCI) was born to create a new interface that allows people with motor disabilities control electronic devices (PC, Smartphone, Smart TV, etc.) or other applications that will be helpful in daily life and provide them more independence. These motor disabilities may be degenerative diseases that gradually loses the ability to move as Amyotrophic Lateral Sclerosis ALS [1], muscular dystrophy, or some type of trauma usually caused by accidents that reduce their motor skills (muscle paralysis, brain injury or bone marrow, limb amputation, etc.)

© Springer Nature Switzerland AG 2020
M. J. Abásolo et al. (Eds.): jAUTI 2019, CCIS 1202, pp. 119–133, 2020.
https://doi.org/10.1007/978-3-030-56574-9_8

BCI systems are devices that interpret and translate thoughts or intensions through electrical signals generated by the user when performing cognitive movements or signals, for this reason these devices are used for artificial intelligence applications, however, artificial intelligence consists in having a computer that simulates the process of human reasoning with its own learning, while a BCI device has an interaction between machine and user.

So a BCI device can be very helpful for user-machine interaction applications, because through control commands, the devices can be manipulated, such as simple applications like: increase, decrease the volume, change channels on a TV, manipulate basic programs on a computer, Tablet, or Smart TV; as well as something more complex such as: interactive applications within a TV, Social Networks (Facebook, Twitter, Instagram), YouTube, or shopping online, take control of computer, among others.

For this reason, this paper looks for a TV remote control implementation using a BCI device, the implementation is carried out using programming tools that comes to link the device and the TV, also it has a graphical interface developed for people manipulation through cognitive signals (gestures or movements). Finally, this work shows the results of evaluation tests focused on improve and have an optimal device that will be used by several people.

2   Brain Computer Interface System Analysis

Brain-Computer Interface is not a new science, the study began in 1929, the first test signals electroencephalogram (EEG), and was used primarily by doctors and scientists to investigate the functioning of the brain. Moving forward with the study proceeded to decode the EEG signals, and to know the intentions so that a person could control certain devices from their brain activity.

So, BCI is defined as a communication system that monitors brain activity and translates specific characteristics corresponding to the intentions of the user, in command of a control device. Under this definition, the BCI systems can be very useful for dependent, elderly or severely disabled people and thus becomes a new communication channel [2].

2.1   BCI Existing Devices

- Neurosky: Device mainly based on the study of EEG signals using bio-sensors, electro-cardiogram's biometric algorithms (ECG) which allow for monitoring and analyzing a wide range of cardio-bio-signals which is not available in other devices [3].
- Emotiv: Device that handles EEG signals that are generated by the human brain, allowing visualization and operation of these signals [4].
- g.Nautilus: device specifically focused on the clinical and medical, developed by researchers, engineers [5].
- Mindball: A device that analyzes the Alpha and Theta signals through a game where tranquility and relaxation of people are manipulated [6].

Table 1. Features BCI devices.

BCI devices				
Mindwave [7]	Emotiv Epoc	Emotiv Epoc insight	Emotiv Epoc flex	Open BCI helmet
Headphone, an ear and a sensor arm Bluetooth connectivity Platforms iOS, Android, PC and Mac EGG emits power spectra (Alpha and Beta) related to care and meditation. It also recognizes the eye blinks AAA battery lasts 8 h Neurosky company It costs around $100 Comfort: Good	14 EEG channels Bluetooth connectivity Rechargeable and motion sensors 9 axes Windows, Mac OS, iOS Sensor Technology: good Cost around $799 Data quality: High Location sensors: Fixed Comfort: Good Emotiv company Preparation time: 3–5 min Private license	5-channel EEG. Bluetooth connectivity Rechargeable and motion sensors 9 axes Sensor Technology: High Cost about $299 Data quality: good Location sensors: Fixed Comfort: Good Emotiv company Preparation time: 1–2 min Private license	32 EEG channels, bluetooth connectivity Private license Sensor technology: higher Cost around $1699 Data quality: configurable Location sensors: configurable Comfort: Good Emotiv company. Preparation time: 15–30 min Private license	8 input channels EEG Sampling frequency up KHz Bluetooth and wireless connection SD card slot to store the session Open Source Priced around $349.99

2.2 Methods Used by BCI

BCI is based on a variety of invasive and non-invasive methods which record activity and brain function, among these are EEG, electrocorticography (ECoG), magnetoencephalography (MEG), positron emission tomography (Positron Emission Tomography, PET) or functional magnetic resonance imaging (functional magnetic resonance Imaging fMRI). Therefore, the most used method for recording brain activity is the EEG BCI systems because it is a simple, non-invasive, portable and low-cost technique [2] (Table 1).

2.3   Internal Operation of a BCI System

BCI systems are made up of a generic functional model shown in Fig. 1, where the basic operation and system process is showed.

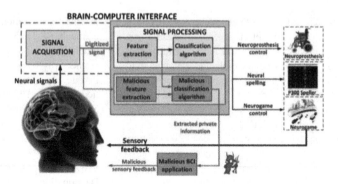

Fig. 1. General structure of a BCI system.

Signal acquisition: records and processes the brain activity of the user.

Signal processing: receives the digitized signal transformed into commands that the device understands. Within this process the signal through several steps such as: noise filtering, obtaining, extraction and translation features.

Application or control interface: functional unit which receives control commands and performs corresponding actions in the device through the same controller [8].

3   Tools Used for the Design and Implementation of the Control Interface

3.1   Hardware and Software of the Project

The software was developed in two environments or IDE's, the first part on "Processing", it permits to communicate between the BCI helmet device and the computer, with a visual interface. The second part was carried out in the "Arduino" environment, where the programming of the button functions and the signals that will be sent to the television was carried out. Arduino libraries were also used for sending and receiving infrared signals, it is available on its GitHub page [9].

On other hand for the hardware we used: Arduino Mega, VS1838B infrared receiver, which allows the decoding of the buttons on the remote control, IR transceiver LED which emits the signal to the television in the project [10].

3.2   Description of the Structure of the System Implemented

The implemented system is formed in four stages as shown in Fig. 2.

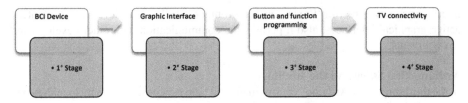

Fig. 2. Stages of the project structure implemented.

EMOTIV graphical environment (1st Stage)

The BCI device for EEG signals that was used in this project is the EMOTIV EPOC +, because of his better comfort, an average of 14 sensors that allow signal acquisition, wireless connectivity that allows to be used without cables, and his price, it's cheaper than others devices on the market. The EMOTIV EPOC + device has its own software, which can be downloaded from the official EMOTIV, in the installation process it offers a series of tabs or modes with tools to familiarize and operate the device. The main interface of the EMOTIV contains 5 tabs or recognition modes, these modes are: status signal, expressive mode, affective mode, cognitive mode, and mouse emulator. Two modes (expressive, cognitive) have the EmoKey configuration, where some expression of the face or movement is configured in a programmed action, such as sending a character, number, or any keyboard combination (ctrl +, alt +, among others) [11] (Fig. 3).

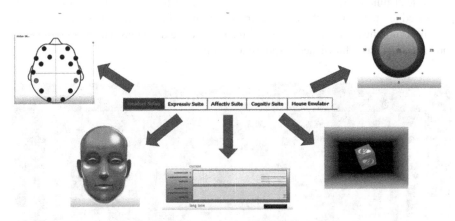

Fig. 3. Mode or tabs on the EMOTIV interface.

GUI "Processing" (2nd Stage)

The BCI device needs to communicate with the computer, for this process a graphical interface was performed. It contains the remote control buttons representing action. The interface was developed on "Processing" environment, it allows the development of interactive graphical interfaces, also it permits the communication with other development environments.

Arduino (3rd Stage and the 4th Stage)

In the third stage, the "Arduino" environment will help us with connectivity to television, where all the functions of the TV remote control buttons are programmed. And libraries to send the infrared signal will be installed.

In the final stage for TV connectivity, Arduino provides modules that are used with the receiver and transmitter for communication with any television having an infrared receiver.

4   Methodology and Implementation of the Gestures and Movements for the Device

To determine the appropriate methodology, an analysis that includes several preliminary tests was made to find out the most common gestures that will be implemented within the project. However, it is known that the gestures in each person can be different, especially on disabled people. For example, some people can only wink left or right, and if they have disabilities, it must be taken into account, which movements or gestures can be executed more easily. For this, tests were carried out with gestures or movement and it was determined how accurate the signal emitted at the time of the action was. We proceeded to qualify with three qualifying terms: true, false or false positive, and at the end observing the results that shown in Fig. 4, make the decisions which are more exact and precise or have the wished response at that time.

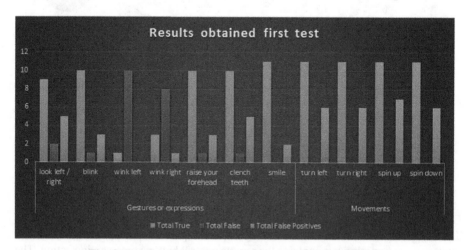

Fig. 4. Results of gestures and movements on the BCI device.

Observing the figure with the gestures and movements results, there are gestures that are easier to detect and other gestures that cannot be detected due to the difficulty to execute. Also, the detection has a good response with the head movements. For these movements is required a training time (5 or 10 min approx.) for greater detection accuracy, while the device can also be trained to learn natural expressions and forced expressions (Table 2).

Table 2. Gestures and button functions of the TV remote control.

Buttons	Movements/Gestures
Volume +	Turn head upwards
Volume −	Turn head down
Channel +	Turn head to the right
Channel −	Turn head to the left
On/off	Wink right or left
Menu	Forehead lift
Up arrow	Turn the head upwards
Down arrow	Turn the head down
Left arrow	Turn head to the right
Down arrow	Turn head to the left
Mute	Look left or right
Back	Teeth
Okay	Unblinking
Activating functions colors	Smile
Red button	Turn head to the left
Green button	Turn head down
Yellow button	Turn head to the right
Blue button	Turn head upwards

Based on these results, gestures representing each button within the application were defined, taking into account that they can vary or change in the moment when the project will be completely integrated.

5 Analysis of the Results

5.1 Final Implementation

Once the corresponding analysis of everything that will be part of the implementation was made, software and hardware, gestures and head movements to be used within our project, we proceeded to the implementation of each of the components and devices on a single project, as shown in Fig. 5.

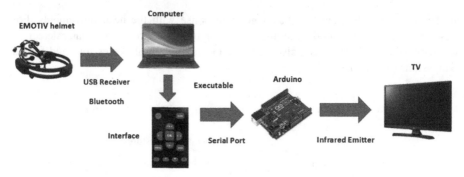

Fig. 5. Total implemented project.

As seen in the previous figure, the EMOTIV device communicates with the computer through an USB port. The interface made in "Processing" was exported to an executable application that communicates with the Arduino. On this device the decoded program will be used to send the IR remote buttons to the TV.

The graphic interface made in "Processing" has the appearance of a TV remote control, with the main buttons (volume, channel, off, mute, menu, back, among others) representing the actions to be performed on the TV (Fig. 6).

Fig. 6. Graphical interface for displaying the actions taken by the person.

5.2 Analysis of Usability Testing

When we had the complete project, with all the components and their connected stages, we proceed to make tests based on the Likert scale [12]. Considering that this scale will allow us to know some details and problems with the use of the project. With the first tests, it is a matter of knowing if there are problems or changes from what was initially proposed, that is, if the gestures are indicated for each action, therefore, a group of 10 people was taken, including children, youth and adults, where was looked for the way to interaction of each other with the project and at the end carry out a survey to be able to have results and present them.

To know the satisfaction of the implemented device, within the quiz there are questions related to topics like: the satisfaction and behavior with the BCI device used, the liking of the graphical interface, the learning of gestures or movements, the calibration time of the gesture sensitivity in each person, and to analyze their rating, 5 rating parameters were taken as: Very Bad, Bad, Regular, Good, Very Good and thus be able to have results and be able to represent them in graphs for be analyzed and know where to optimize or try to improve.

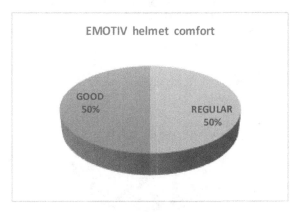

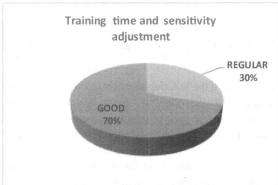

Fig. 7. Result of comfort, time and setting helmet EMOTIV.

Figure 7 shows the result where even seen that the helmet after a time of approximately 1 h of operation comes to give some discomfort with some people but not necessarily all because many times the sponge's sensor dry out and that causes the trouble, but it can solve by hydrating the sensors again. While on the part of training and sensitivity setting of gestures and movements widely accepted by people, where that was explained that it takes time in the cognitive way to get to train helmet and a little sensitivity adjustment in the expressive mode.

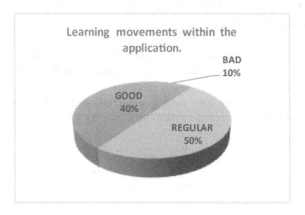

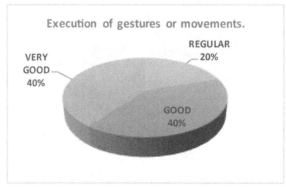

Fig. 8. Result of learning and execution of gestures or movements in the project.

Figure 8 shows the result of the learning and execution of gestures within the project, because of it, we could know that there are many gestures and movements that are difficult to use, generating a memorize problem for the people. It could also visualize many gestures generate unwanted actions and therefore not the optimal functioning of the project.

The results showed in Fig. 9, are about the display of the graphical interface, the size of the letters buttons, among other presentation characteristics, given an acceptable response, also we have several changes recommendations, such as the size of the interface, larger letters of the interface window; but in general here we have a well-accepted context of implementation.

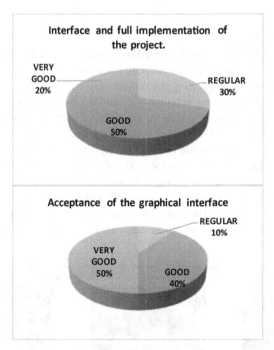

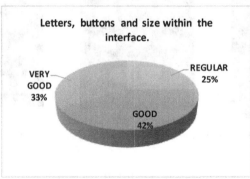

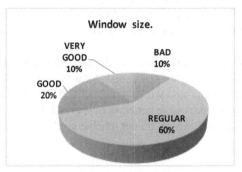

Fig. 9. Results of the visual project part, graphical interface and physical implementation.

6 Discussion

The tests with the entire project implemented were carried out between men and women, where the predetermined gestures and movements were tested, in order to have results, opinions and comments when testing the project, and to know the problems that exist and to be able to solve them. One problem was the false positives at the time of making the gestures, sometimes without having the intention of using the device, it was already receiving gestures, in order to solve this, a validation and activation of the control was carried out, with this it was possible to avoid false positives that initially occurred.

The validation or activation is done by two head movement, one movement or turn to the left + one movement or turn to the right, with these two actions the remote control of the application will enter into operation, giving 15 s of lapse time, that was determined with the first tests, within this time any TV action is allowed. At the end of this lapse time you must execute the activation movements again to be able to use the TV (Fig. 10).

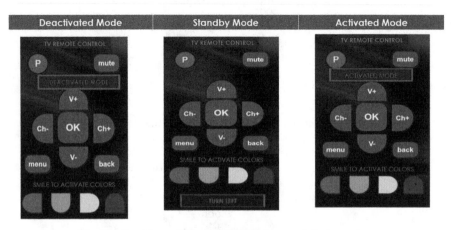

Fig. 10. Graphic user interface with changes and final warnings.

In addition, with the results showed in Fig. 9, we visualized that we have too many gestures and that is difficult for the user, therefore we minimized gestures to main gestures, to have a use with less errors and checking whether the project works successfully (Table 3).

After carrying out the tests with the gestures already minimized and the activation that was proposed to minimize errors, we proceeded to carry out the final tests and analyze the results by asking the people who wore the helmet and used the project (Fig. 11).

As it can see, the final results were better; people could do more easily actions with the project, and use of gestures which are not much complicated in testing.

Table 3. Main buttons TV with their gestures.

Buttons	Movements/Gestures
Volume +	Turn up
Volume −	Turn down
Canal +	Rotate right
Channel −	Turn left toward
On (On)/Off	Wink right or left

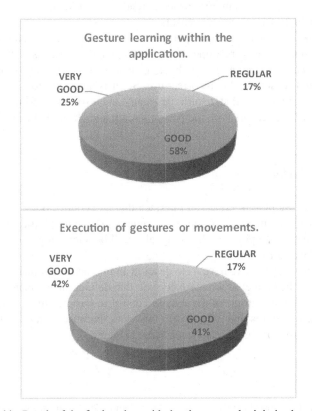

Fig. 11. Result of the final project with the changes and minimized gestures.

7 Conclusions

The implementation and realization of a television remote control interface using BCI technology was successful and fulfilled the objective. This project becomes a solution for people who have motor disabilities or degenerative diseases in their upper extremities, they can manipulate and interact with a TV, through a remote control. So the project defined an adequate methodology to choose the gestures or movements of the head, so that people can do actions on TV, including personalized form, knowing the situation of the person, that is to say, not all people will be able doing some gestures or movements and depending that, the gestures and movements will be programmed; The tests carried out served to detect the main problems with gestures and some difficulties that can be had with each person, this gave way to define the proposed methodology.

Working with EEG signals is very complex, especially trying to be exact with the signals produced by each person, and this has been verified within the project when using BCI devices, we cannot have a predetermined training or sensitivity adjustment in the same way, because each person has different signals or gestures, and therefore it is difficult to get to control devices in an exact way, and within these projects it is taken into account that we can get, with more sensors a greater accuracy, but since has mentioned the cost will be high if we use more sensors.

It was verified within the helmet operation tests, that there are several interferences that produce errors in the correct operation, these can be: noise caused by the environment, the incorrect positioning of the helmet, the incorrect contact of the sensor with the scalp or oxidized sensors by the incorrect use. So, it is necessary to have a controlled environment without noises that disturb the signal, and also it is important to prove the correct contact of the sensors with the person's scalp and check that each sensor is not rusting.

8   Future Works

For future works we plan to create an interface that can control other devices such as PC, smartphones, etc., making it easier for people who have difficulties handling these devices because of some physical disability, also will be interesting to complement the helmet using voice commands.

Another future job that we have, is to develop an interactive application for TV that can be used with the helmet as a remote control, that defines an adequate methodology in order to reduce the buttons on the remote control to basic or main buttons, and so helping to reduce gestures that are found in this work, because with more gestures that are used, more errors or signals can occur in the helmet.

References

1. Mayo Clinic: Esclerosis lateral amiotrófica, 14 Diciembre 2019. https://www.mayoclinic.org/es-es/diseases-conditions/amyotrophic-lateral-sclerosis/symptoms-causes/syc-20354022
2. Hornero, R., Corralejo, R., Álvarez, D.: Brain-Computer Interface (BCI) aplicado al entrenamiento cognitivo y control domótico para prevenir los efectos del envejecimiento, Marzo 2012. http://www.fgcsic.es/lychnos/es_es/articulos/Brain-Computer-Interface-aplicado-al-entrenamiento-cognitivo. Accessed 15 May 2019
3. Neurosky: Neurosky Body and Mind. Quantified (2018). http://neurosky.com/about-neurosky/
4. EMOTIV: EMOTIV About us (2018). https://www.emotiv.com/about-emotiv/
5. g.tec: g.Nautilus (2018). http://www.gtec.at/Products/Hardware-and-Accessories/g.Nautilus-Specs-Features

6. ALVY: microsiervos, 18 Abril 2018. https://www.microsiervos.com/archivo/juegos-y-divers ion/mindball.html
7. NeuroSky: Mindwave mobile 2 (2018). https://store.neurosky.com/pages/mindwave
8. Gutiérrez Martinez, J., Cantillo Negrete, J., Cariño Escobar, R., Elías Viñas, D.: Los sistemas de interfaz cerebro-computadora, Mayo–Agosto 2013. https://www.medigraphic.com/pdfs/invdis/ir-2013/ir132c.pdf
9. Adafruit: Recepción y decodificacion IR, 26 Febrero 2015. https://learn.adafruit.com/using-an-infrared-library/hardware-needed#
10. Adafruit: Envio de codigo IR, 26 Febrero 2015. https://learn.adafruit.com/using-an-infrared-library/sending-ir-codes
11. EMOTIV: User Manual EMOTIV (2018)
12. Sánchez, F.M.A.: Psicología Social Aplicada. Pearson Educación S.A, Madrid (2002)

ICT Oriented to the Elderly and Their Active Aging: A Systematic Review

Magdalena Rosado[1](✉) ⓘ, María J. Abásolo[2,3](✉) ⓘ, and Telmo Silva[4](✉) ⓘ

[1] Faculty of Medical Sciences, Catholic University of Santiago de Guayaquil, Guayaquil, Ecuador
maria.rosadoa@info.unlp.edu.ar
[2] Faculty of Informatics, National University of La Plata (UNLP), La Plata, Argentina
mjabasolo@lidi.info.unlp.edu.ar
[3] CICPBA Scientific Research Commission of the Buenos Aires Province, La Plata, Argentina
[4] University of Aveiro, Aveiro, Portugal
tsilva@ua.pt

Abstract. This work presents a systematic review, from 2012 to the beginning of 2019, of experiences carried out with people over 65 years old, using Information and Communication Technologies (ICT) with the aim of improving their self-care and health care empowerment for active aging. Most of the analyzed studies are focused on monitoring and assistance of older adults, meanwhile there are a minority of studies focused on rehabilitation. The most used ICT for health care are mobile applications and web services. Also there is a prevalence of use of specific sensors to monitor or control older adults. In relation with the promotion of exercises, the main purpose is the prevention of falls of older adults. Few projects used Interactive Television with solutions that allow older adults to easily set reminders for their health care and use entertainment programs to have physical, mental and social well-being. Particularly we found very few projects related to promote physical activity.

Keywords: Older adult · Active aging · Technology · Health platforms · Digital television · iTV · ICT

1 Introduction

The life expectancy of the older adult is growing, and given the need to guarantee the good quality of life of older people, there are several actions that are being taken to promote health and active aging. Active aging is defined by the World Health Organization (WHO 2015) as "the process of optimizing health, participation and safety opportunities in order to improve the quality of life of people as they age". There are four fundamental pillars that promote it such as healthy nutrition, physical activity, prevention and social behavior. In relation to these pillars, nutrition is said to play a very important role in the aging process because muscle mass is lost due to multiple diseases typical of age, alongside with the loss of dental pieces, which generates a difficulty in digestion and

© Springer Nature Switzerland AG 2020
M. J. Abásolo et al. (Eds.): jAUTI 2019, CCIS 1202, pp. 134–155, 2020.
https://doi.org/10.1007/978-3-030-56574-9_9

absorption of nutrients. Regarding physical activity, it is beneficial for health, helps to reduce pain, discomfort, and prevents the development of diseases. Preventive activities in older adults must be taken into account so that their health does not deteriorate. For there to be successful and healthy aging, there must be social and family integration of those who are aging. This would imply highlighting the social and cultural challenges that still continue and make it impossible for older adults to develop their potential.

Aging represents the greatest challenge of the 21st century with the promotion of active and healthy aging through Information and Communication Technologies (ICT) contributing to the independent life of the elderly. For (Castrillón et al. 2010) the impact of technological and social innovation is acknowledged in the actions, facts and activities that produce changes in behaviors, attitudes and social practices, which implies changes in them, to solve problems, deficiencies or own/collective needs. The use of technology constitutes advances that represent positive changes in people in the development of their activities in their daily lives, making their practice easier, simpler, more pleasant and more comfortable when they are carried out.

ICT have a wide potential for support in the health field, providing computer services that facilitate the exchange of information and enable access to knowledge about a variety of medical treatments and practices (Martínez-Alcalá et al. 2015), as well as remote treatment systems allow people to remain independent in their own homes. The benefits of this digital age contribute to provide evaluations that allow applying the most precise assistance for the benefit of the health of the other (de Abreu and Almeida 2014).

Demographic, epidemiological, social and economic changes have generated major changes in lifestyle, type of homes and family dynamics, leading its members to be increasingly involved in the care of older adults (Giraldo-Rodriguez et al. 2013). Agudo-Prado et al. (2012) express that the use of communication technologies with older people opens up great possibilities for intervention, favors the connection and approach of older people to new issues and phenomena that are emerging in society.

Television is an entertainment service, but is can also be applied as a self-service server for the person who is at home. In accordance with what is proposed (Pùrez-Ugena y Coromina et al. 2009), from a social perspective, the fact that a device helps the elderly to remain in their homes with complete independence is an important social achievement.

This article presents a systematic review on the use of technology to improve self-care and health care empowerment of older adults for active aging. Section 2 describes the methodology used for this systematic review. Section 3 shows the extraction of information of the selected studies. Section 4 shows the results highlighting the main outcomes of each study. Finally Sect. 5 presents conclusions and future work.

2 Methodology

The systematic review requires a research process with the objective of obtaining, evaluating and interpreting clearly, precisely, rigorously and methodically all the information that is related to a research question. For this study, the used method has been proposed by Kitchenham (2004) consisting of six steps followed: (i) Formulation of the question; (ii) Search for sources; (iii) Selection of studies using the inclusion and exclusion criteria; (iv) Extraction of information; (v) Presentation of the results; (vi) Discussion.

2.1 Formulation of the Questions

For more than a decade, the rapid growth that ICTs has become an opportunity for the elderly to be involved with the appropriation technologies processes, and its benefits at the personal, familiar and social levels. In this context the research team tried to answer the following research questions:

PI 1. What are the ICT recently used to help older adults to take care of their health?

PI 2. For what purpose are these tools used?

PI 3. Where were the experiences carried out? What methodology was applied? Which stage of development was reached?

PI 4. What results were obtained in experiencies focused in health care through physical exercises?

PI 5. How Digital Interactive Television (iTV) is used to help older adults to take care of their health and particularly through physical exercise?

2.2 Source Search

A bibliographic search was carried out in different scientific databases such as: ACM Digital Library, Scopus, Springer and Google Scholar. The search was performed in April 2019, and full articles were selected, available and published from 2012 to the beginning of 2019. For the search, descriptors in Health Sciences (DeHS) present in the title and abstract of the articles were used. Search strings used were: (Technology AND Health AND Elderly AND Exercise); (Interactive AND Television AND Health AND Elderly).

2.3 Selection of Studies Using the Inclusion and Exclusion Criteria

The keyword search presented above yielded a result of 573 articles. Exclusion and inclusion criteria were applied in three stages as follows (Table 1).

Table 1. Search results and application of selection criteria

Search string	Source	Found	No duplicated	Meet inclusion criteria	Meet exclusion criteria
Technology AND Health AND Elderly AND Exercise	ACM Digital Library	58	32	16	17
	Google Scholar	132	33	9	5
	Springer	102	26	5	8
	Scopus	48	6	4	3
Interactive Television AND Health AND Elderly	ACM Digital Library	37	16	3	1
	Google Scholar	68	22	7	6
	Springer	48	39	9	6
	Scopus	80	36	13	2
Total		573	210	66	48

Table 2. Results by search string

Search string	Related authors
Technology AND Health AND Elderly AND Exercise	Vuorimaa et al. (2012), Hamid and Foong (2012), Park et al. (2014), Nazário et al. (2015), Ojetola et al. (2015), Suyama (2016), Ren et al. (2016), Anastasiou et al. (2016), Dulva Hina et al. (2016), Lo Bianco et al. (2016), Tsiachri Renta et al. (2017), Suyama (2017), Palipana et al. (2018), Matthies et al. (2018), Sáenz-de-Urturi and Santos (2018), Urbauer et al. (2018), Parvin et al. (2018), Trujillo et al. (2013), Cisneros Perdomo et al. (2015), Muntaner et al. (2016), Netto and Tateyama (2018), Toribio-Guzmán et al. (2018), Lasheng et al. (2012), Tseng et al. (2013), Molina et al. (2014), Johnson et al. (2014), Palacio et al. (2017), Kyriazakos et al. (2017), Al-khafajiy et al. (2019), Rao (2019), Konstantinidis et al. (2016), Luna-García (2015), Saracchini (2015)
Interactive Television AND Elderly	Godard et al. (2013), Aal et al.(2014), Silva et al. (2014), Añaños (2015), Blanco (2016), Santana-Mancilla and Anido-Rifón (2017), Ribeiro et al. (2018), Picking et al. (2012), Spinsante and Gambi (2012), Stojmenova et al. (2013), Epelde et al. (2013), Miyoshi et al. (2015), Orso et al. (2017), Scandurra and Sjölinder (2013), Santana and Anido (2016)

First, the articles that don't not contain any communication were removed. We keep the article that offered relevant details for this exploration from several publications that came from these same research. After applying these exclusion criteria, 210 articles remained. Second, the articles were included if they present the development or implementation of ICT used to help older adults to grant themselves self-care to improve their health, applied for active aging, care-type, monitoring or rehabilitation. Furthermore, the studies must have been carried out with people 65 years or older. After that the number of articles was reduced to 66. Finally, a second process of exclusion was applied, discarding articles related with more specific target population - like special cases of physiological aging, degenerative diseases of the nervous system, mental, osteoarticular- with special care by conventional portable tools to monitor vital functions, clinical parameters, etc. The result of the application of previous mentioned filters results in a selection of 48 articles presented in Table 2.

3 Extraction of Information

To answer the research questions, the following information was extracted from each of the 48 selected publication (see Table 3):

- Purpose of application: assistance (A) when it comes to interactive solutions to help the older adult to do their tasks and activities, leading them to have higher levels of well-being; monitoring (M), when it comes to a solution capable of observing and assisting older people remotely; and rehabilitation (R) when it comes to solutions that help to change the sedentary behavior of the older adult through daily exercises or routine.
- Methodology of the experience: qualitative, quantitative or mixed;
- Applied technology;
- Development Status: implemented application (I), feasibility study (FS), prototype (P).
- Also the country where the study was carried out was taken into account.

There were extracted 13 studies in which ICT contribute to active and healthy aging through exercise. Table 4 presents the objectives and the results obtained in each study, except two of the studies that use iTV that were included in the next table.

There were also extracted other 13 studies that particularly use iTV applications for older adults to take care of their health, of which the objectives and the results obtained were presented in Table 5. Two of the studies, that are highlighted in gray, particularly promote physical exercise.

Table 3. Selected experiences purpose, methodology, country, technology and status of development

Reference	Purpose	Methodology	Country	Technology	Status
Lasheng et al. (2012)	A	Qualitative	China	Sensors – Mobile device	FS
Vuorimaa et al. (2012)	A	Mixed	Finland	Cloud - PC	FS
Hamid and Foong (2012)	A	Mixed	Singapore	Mobile device	P
Picking et al. (2012)	A	Mixed	Wales, United Kingdom	Set Top Box - Sensors – Interactive TV	FS
Spinsante and Gambi (2012)	M	Mixed	Italy	Interactive TV – Mobile device	I
Tseng et al. (2013)	M	Mixed	Taiwan	Cloud - Sensors- Mobile device - PC	I

(continued)

Table 3. (*continued*)

Reference	Purpose	Methodology	Country	Technology	Status
Scandurra and Sjölinder (2013)	A	Mixed	Sweden	Interactive TV – Mobile device	I
Godard et al. (2013)	A	Mixed	France, Finland	Kinect- Interactive television- Mobile device	P
Trujillo et al. (2013)	M	Mixed	Colombia	Kinect - Set Top Box – Mobile device - PC	P
Stojmenova et al. (2013)	A	Mixed	Slovenia	Cloud - Sensors – Interactive TV – Mobile device - PC	P
Epelde (2013)	M	Mixed	Spain, Germany, United Kingdom	Sensors- Interactive TV –Mobile device- PC	I
Aal et al. (2014)	M	Mixed	Germany, Spain, Australia	Cloud – Interactive TV – Mobile device	P
Molina et al. (2014)	R	Mixed	USA, Brazil, Portugal, Australia, Canada	Kinect - Cloud - Sensors	FS
Johnson et al. (2014)	M	Mixed	Netherlands, Italy, Germany, Austria	Cloud -Sensors – Mobile device - Bluetooth	P
Silva et al. (2014)	A	Mixed	Portugal	Interactive TV	P
Park et al. (2014)	M	Mixed	South Korea	Sensors – Mobile device	P
Konstantinidis et al. (2016)	R	Mixed	Greece	Headphones – Sensors - PC	I
Miyoshi et al. (2015)	R	Mixed	Japan	Interactive TV – Mobile device	P
Nazário et al. (2015)	M	Mixed	Brazil	Cloud - Sensors- Mobile device	I
Ojetola et al. (2015)	M	Mixed	England, United Kingdom	Sensors – Mobile device - Bluetooth	I
Añaños (2015)	M	Mixed	Spain	Cloud – Interactive TV- Mobile device	I

(*continued*)

Table 3. (*continued*)

Reference	Purpose	Methodology	Country	Technology	Status
Cisneros Perdomo et al. (2015)	R	Mixed	Cuba	PC	FS
Luna-García (2015)	A	Mixed	Mexico	PC	I
Saracchini (2015)	A	Mixed	Spain	Cloud - set Top Box – Interactive TV – Mobile device	I
Suyama (2016)	A	Mixed	Japan	Cloud - Sensors – Mobile device- Bluetooth	FS
Ren et al. (2016)	M	Mixed	Netherlands	Cloud – Sensors – Mobile device	P
Anastasiou et al. (2016)	M	Mixed	Greece	Mobile device	I
Dulva Hina et al. (2016)	M	Mixed	France	Mobile device	I
Lo Bianco et al. (2016)	M	Qualitative	Australia	Sensors - Mobile device - Bluetooth	P
Santana and Anido (2016)	A	Mixed	Mexico, Spain	Interactive TV	P
Blanco (2016)	M	Mixed	Spain	Sensors – Interactive TV- Bluetooth	I
Muntaner et al. (2016)	M	Mixed	Spain	Cloud - Sensors - Mobile device - Bluetooth	FS
Santana-Mancilla and Anido-Rifón (2017)	M	Mixed	Mexico	Set Top Box – Interactive TV	P
Palacio et al. (2017)	M	Mixed	Mexico	Kinect – Cloud - Sensors – Mobile device	FS
Kyriazakos et al. (2017)	M	Mixed	Austria, Italy, Denmark, Netherlands	Cloud - Mobile device	I
Renta et al. (2017)	A	Mixed	Greece, Canada	Cloud - Sensors- Mobile device	I

(*continued*)

Table 3. (*continued*)

Reference	Purpose	Methodology	Country	Technology	Status
Ribeiro et al. (2018)	A	Mixed	Portugal	Kinect - Cloud - Sensors – Interactive TV - Mobile device – Software - PC	P
Suyama (2016)	A	Mixed	Japan	Cloud – Sensors - Mobile device - Bluetooth	I
Orso et al. (2017)	A	Mixed	Spain, Italy	Set Top Box - Sensors –Interactive TV - PC	P
Palipana et al. (2018)	M	Mixed	Ireland	Sensors – Mobile device – Bluetooth	P
Matthies et al. (2018)	M	Mixed	Germany, New Zealand	Sensors - Mobile device - Bluetooth	P
Sáenz-de-Urturi and Santos (2018)	R	Mixed	Spain	Kinect - Cloud- Sensors - Mobile device	I
Urbauer et al. (2018)	A	Mixed	Austria	Sensors - Mobile device - Bluetooth	P
Parvin et al. (2018)	A	Quantitative	Italy	Cloud - Sensors - Mobile device - Bluetooth	I
Netto and Tateyama (2018)	A	Mixed	Brazil	Cloud - Sensors - Mobile device	P
Toribio-Guzmán et al. (2018)	R	Mixed	Spain	PC	I
Al-khafajiy et al. (2019)	M	Mixed	England, United Kingdom	Cloud - Sensors - Mobile device -Bluetooth	I
Rao (2019)	M	Mixed	USA	Sensors	FS

Table 4. Characterization of articles that promote physical exercise

Ref.	Topic	Aim	Result
Rao (2019)	Portable sensor technology to measuring physical activity (PA) in the elderly	Research the use of wearable devices to measure physical activities of older adults	To measure physical activity they use multiple types of sensors, including pedometers, uniaxial, biaxial and triaxial accelerometers, heart rate monitors combined with accelerometers, complex systems and that need to improve precision of the measurement type, the spatial extent of physical activity, being necessary to develop clear standards for measurement, algorithms used to calculate clinically relevant measurements
Molina et al. (2014)	Virtual reality using games to improve physical functioning in older adults: a systematic review	Study the effectiveness of virtual reality in games for physical functioning in older adults	A summary of the effects of exergames in improving physical functioning in older adults, the results of the studies were analyzed with the PEDro scale, reflecting that most of the studies presented methodological problems and that other studies were necessary to achieve better methodological quality, external validity to provide stronger scientific evidence
Ojetola et al. (2015)	Dataset for Fall Events and Daily Activities from Inertial Sensors	Develop a fall detection system using sensors	Protocols for falls in real time through a machine learning algorithm, where the results showed that the algorithm was able to discriminate between falls and life activities (ADL) with an F measure 94%
Palipana et al. (2018)	FallDeFi: Ubiquitous Fall Detection Using Commodity Wi-Fi Devices	Develop a fall detection system using WiFi sensors	Comparison of various algorithms for estimating body characteristics to select the most optimal. Then, through a study, a case of a threshold-based fall detection system was illustrated to know the algorithms for estimating body characteristics, demonstrating that the algorithm is effective in detecting falls

(*continued*)

Table 4. (*continued*)

Ref.	Topic	Aim	Result
Ren et al. (2016)	FLOW Pillow: Exploring Sitting, experience towards active aging	Develop an innovative app to allow exercise in older adults	By FLOW pillow, older people could have an immersive experience to do low intensity when exercising, since the light weight of the pillow, allowed to improve the mobility and flexibility of the Flow system. Regardless of the relatively small size (40 * 40 cm^2), most of the participants gave positive comments about the use of the pillow to support their exercise
Dulva Hina et al. (2016)	Serious game: autonomy and better health for the elderly	Develop a game that promotes physical and mental activities in older adults	Playing serious games for the elderly in a month allowed to improve the autonomy and health of older people who do not perform many physical activities and mental challenges
Lo Bianco et al. (2016)	A perspective of the health industry on augmented reality as a communication tool in the prevention of falls in the elderly	Using Augmented Reality to prevent falls in older adults	The professionals in the prevention industry foresee augmented reality as a clinical design tool that allows the prevention of falls, and that the use of this tool would improve the provision of customer services
Cisneros Perdomo et al. (2015)	Efficacy of the Cobs platform in balance, posture and gait disorders in the elderly	Evaluate usability of Cobs application in older adults	Results of exercises in older adults with balance, posture and gait disorders with the Cobs platform, which is an informative response and training team with information represented graphically, acoustically or both, in real time, on the movements of the body, showing effective in the therapy performed to an experimental group and to the control group, clinical treatment was performed without changes in functional condition disorders

(*continued*)

Table 4. (*continued*)

Ref.	Topic	Aim	Result
Muntaner et al. (2016)	Effects of a face-to-face training program vs. prescription through a mobile application in older people	Compare the effectiveness of a physical program with a mobile remote application	The results suggest that a 10-week intervention administered in person and based on physical exercise is more effective than the same intervention prescribed through a mobile application, in relation to cardiovascular parameters
Trujillo et al. (2013)	Exergames: a technological tool for physical activity	Determine the feasibility of using exergames as a physical activity tool	With the use of exergames, 98% of users see the use of interactive systems as an alternative to carry out a directed, personalized routine, making the time for physical activity more enjoyable
Konstantinidis et al. (2016)	Design, implementation and extensive pilot implementation of FitForAll: an easy-to-use exercise platform	Analyze the usability of the FitForAll platform (FFA), user adherence to exercise, and design effectiveness	The elderly who use the FitForAll (FFA) platform significantly improved strength, flexibility, endurance and balance while presenting a significant trend in quality of life improvements

Table 5. Characterization of the articles on iTV

Ref.	Topic	Aim	Result
Santana-Mancilla and Anido-Rifón (2017)	Technological acceptance of a TV platform for older people living alone or in public nursing homes	Develop an iTV application that serves as a reminder for older adults	Adoption of this iTV application was very acceptable to its target audience, which allowed them to have greater control over daily activities
Aal et al. (2014)	A fall prevention iTV solution for older adults	Design a training system to predict and prevent falls in older adults	Through the ICT based training system that offered balance training, strength exercises to predict and prevent falls, the elderly had a positive impact on their quality of life

(*continued*)

Table 5. (*continued*)

Ref.	Topic	Aim	Result
Scandurra and Sjölinder (2013)	Participatory design with older people: Design of the future Services and iterative refinements of interactive eHealth services for older people	Develop an iTV application focused on: cognitive activities, physical activities and social activities	This system made it possible to establish communication between medical personnel/the elderly, the elderly/young, and between the elderly, promoting social inclusion
Silva et al. (2014)	Use of Wizard of Oz Prototype to determine automatic identification methods for older viewers	Promote active aging through the creation of Wizard of Oz (remote control for iTV)	A novel element (Wizard of Oz) is incorporated to facilitate the customization of iTV content
Santana and Anido (2016)	Heuristic evaluation of an interactive television system to facilitate care in the nursing home	Evaluate the usability of iTV applications following a heuristic scale	iTVCare proves to be an interactive application with an intuitive interface that followed heuristic guidelines during the development phase to cope with problems of older adults
Ribeiro et al. (2018)	Application for older adults to ask for help through television: design and evaluation of a high visual fidelity prototype	Create an iTV app that allows volunteering among older adults	The interface design was evaluated in heuristic evaluation sessions and user tests, the former was supported by a list of heuristics, extracted from other schemes used in recent research
Blanco (2016)	Good practices of the Enred@te Pilot Project: digital social network for the elderly and volunteers of the Spanish Red Cross	Promote volunteering through a video-communication application (iTV)	Three profiles: participants, users, volunteers and technicians evaluated the quality of the video communication, when using 4G and 3G

(*continued*)

Table 5. (*continued*)

Ref.	Topic	Aim	Result
Añaños (2015)	The Eye Tracker technology in older adults: how integrated television content is served and processed	Compare the effectiveness of eye tracker in older and younger adults for use on iTV	Older adults had difficulties in processing and recognizing information on iTV compared to young people
Godard et al. (2013)	WeSlide: Gesture text input for older users	Develop a management technique for data entry in iTV	WeSlide was compared with other devices and it is concluded that this text input method is patient friendly
Orso et al. (2017)	Interactive multimedia content for older adults: the case of SeniorChannel	Analyze if SeniorChannel adapts to the needs (for example: usability, accessibility, among others) of older adults	iTV application allowed older adults being active participants by various physical activities. A set of guides for the design of iTV application was presented
Picking et al. (2012)	The Easyline + project: evaluation of a user interface developed to improve the independent life of older people	Assist in the interaction between older adults with kitchen objects	The use of the product followed strict ethical and usability guidelines
Stojmenova et al. (2013)	Assisted living solutions for the elderly through interactive TV	Develop an iTV application capable of reminding older adults about prescription and dosage	The application was user friendly with an intuitive interface
Spinsante and Gambi (2012)	Provide interactive universal access services through televisions: implementation and validation with older users	Develop an iTV application that incorporates new functionalities (videoconference and voice) to assist older adults	Interactive TV application that allows customizing GUI

(*continued*)

Table 5. (*continued*)

Ref.	Topic	Aim	Result
Miyoshi et al. (2015)	Smart home and home rehabilitation training system using interactive television	Develop a TVDi home rehabilitation application for older adults	With a home rehabilitation training system allowed to create a good environment for older people, the training system worked correctly and the results suggested that the participants maintained or improved their physical activity
Epelde (2013)	Provide interactive universal access services through televisions: implementation and validation with users	Develop an iTV application that incorporates new functionalities (videoconference and voice) to assist older adults	Interactive TV application that allows the incorporation of Ambient Intelligence concepts

4   Results

The selected studies has been increasing slightly from 2012 (10%) to 2016 (17%), maintaining in 2017 and 2018 (15% each one) and the percentage of 5% of the first four months of 2019.

The research questions formulated from the findings of the reviewed articles are answered below.

4.1   What Are the ICT Recently Used to Help Older Adults to Take Care of Their Health? (PI 1)

The usage of the different ICT to encourage the elderly to take care of their health extracted from Table 3 is shown in Fig. 1. It can be observed that the three most used ICT are the mobile device, sensors and web platforms for health service. Most of studies use mobile devices (27%), which allow increasing the autonomy of the older adult. Second, 22% of studies use sensors that allow the older adult to move freely with control. Thirdly, 16% of studies use cloud applications. It is possible to verify that 11% of the studies make use of iTV, and 3% use the Set Top Box to present a simple and comfortable interface for use with a television. Other studies (10%) use bluetooth to transmit information between other devices. A minority of 7% use the PC and lastly 4% of the studies used the Kinect camera to capture people's movements.

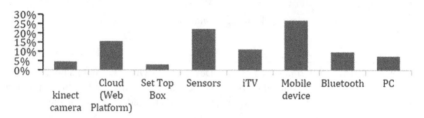

Fig. 1. ICTs used by studies

4.2 For What Purpose Are These Tools Used? (PI 2)

First, with regards to the purpose of the ICTs involved in the studies of Table 3, it can be seen in Fig. 2 that almost half of the studies (47.92%) are focused on monitoring functionality (M), followed by 39.58% on assistance (A) and with a minor percentage of 12.50% on rehabilitation (R).

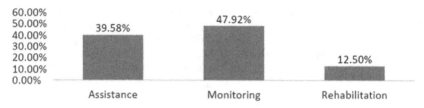

Fig. 2. Selected articles distribution by application type

Particularly the studies that promote physical exercise (Table 4), it can be indicated that 17% focus on the monitoring functionality (M) used to support activity monitoring. automatic, to start and stop a workout; 3% focus in rehabilitation operability (R) with the aim of experiencing positive changes at the physiological level with computerized rehabilitation, which gives the person greater confidence and security.

4.3 Where Were the Experiences Carried Out? What Methodology Was Applied? Which Stage of Development Was Reached? (PI 3)

Distribution

Figure 3 shows distribution of the studies of Table 3 by countries grouped by continents. In some studies several countries or continents were involved. Half of the studies (50%) were developed in European countries (Germany, Denmark, Slovenia, Spain, Finland, France, Wales, Greece, England, Ireland, Italy, Portugal, United Kingdom, Sweden, Austria, and the Netherlands). The 17% of the studies were carried out in American countries (Brazil, Canada, Colombia, Cuba, the United States and Mexico). Asia reached 15% of the studies (China, South Korea, Japan, Singapore and Taiwan). Finally 4% of the studies were in Oceania (Australia, New Zealand). The studies that were carried out in countries of different continents were 8% between America and Europe; 4% Europe and Oceania and 2% America, Europe and Oceania. In these cases, the researchers were looking for different contributions that would make it possible to know the research work and their scientific collaboration for the employment of the elderly in diversity among countries.

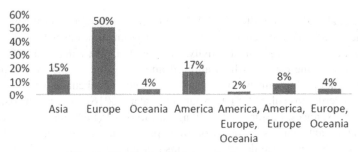

Fig. 3. Distribution of the studies by continent

Methodology
It was observed that in 91% of the studies of Table 3 the researchers applied a mixed approach where they integrate quantitative and qualitative data to support the research, and in 9% of the studies a qualitative research was applied that allowed knowing the reality in its context of application and development.

Stage of Development
Regarding the state of development reached by each study of Table 3, 41.67% of the studies are applications implemented and put into operation in places that allowed follow-up, with the intervention of a multidisciplinary team, including medical personnel and caregivers. The 39.58% of the studies are developed prototypes that still need to incorporate some functionality, so their usefulness or benefit can be proven. Finally, 18.75% refer to feasibility studies in the use of the resources or tools necessary to determine if a group of older adults who suffer from health problems are willing to try a strategy or application that contributes to reintegration into society (Fig. 4).

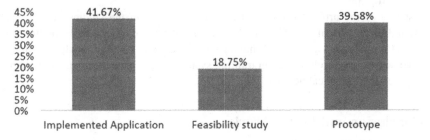

Fig. 4. Distribution of the state of development of the selected articles

4.4 What Results Were Obtained in Experiencies Focused in Health Care Through Physical Exercises? (PI 4)

To answer the question, the articles found in Table 4 are analyzed. Particularly the two studies that use iTV and were included in Table 5 will be commented in the next section (PI 5).

Molina et al. (2014), Trujillo et al. (2013) stimulate the mobility of the whole body through the use of interactive environments and at the same time check how effective the tool is when carrying out physical activity. Meanwhile Dulva Hina et al. (2016) made serious games for the elderly, which allowed improving the autonomy and health of those who do not perform many physical activities and mental challenges.

Cisneros Perdomo et al. (2015), Konstantinidis et al. (2016), assessed the risk of falls with balance exercises, posture and walking on FitForAll (FFA) and Cobs platforms, showing significant changes in quality of life improvements. Ojetola et al. (2015), Palipana et al. (2018) developed detection systems based on protocols and algorithms that when performing exercises identify risk factors and act on them; Lo Bianco et al. (2016) have shown progress in preventing falls by means of exercises with augmented reality.

For Rao (2019) the use of multiple types of sensors allowed to know that when performing physical activity it is necessary to develop clear standards to calculate clinically relevant measurements. Muntaner et al. (2016) emphasizes that when performing exercises there are no differences when doing them in a conventional way than with the mobile application. Ren et al. (2016) point that when performing exercises the Flow pillow allowed to improve mobility and older people's flexibility.

4.5 How Digital Interactive Television (ITV) Is Used to Help Older Adults to Take Care of Their Health? (PI 5)

The iTV studies of Table 5 show that iTV is a significant contribution to prevention and medical care in older adults, which can be extended to different ages of the human being, according to the existing health problem.

More than half of the studies developed systems that allow older adults to easily set reminders, such as time to take their medications and other activities for their health care, so the second majority (27%) of studies make the most of the opportunities that offers entertainment to have physical, mental and social well-being throughout life and television programs.

Just two of the articles used the TVDi for exercises in the studies of Aal et al. (2014) and Miyoshi et al. (2015), who designed solutions for older adults; the first with exercises for prevention against falls having a positive impact on their quality of life and the other with a home rehabilitation training system where the participants maintained or improved their physical activity.

5 Conclusion and Future Work

A review of ICT aiming to enhance older adults' quality of life has been presented. The results allow to know that there is a diversity of solutions ranging from assistance, monitoring, to rehabilitation functionalities. The ICT used are mainly focused on mobile devices, motion sensors, and cloud applications.

The technology adopted to be used by the elderly in health services reflects the practice of self-care, maintaining a balance between the insertion of technological machinery and the maintenance of the humanization of care. The solutions analyzed constitute an important contribution as it helps to improve the quality of life of the elderly through empowerment, showing that technology plays a significant role within the human being at any stage of his life.

Special emphasis was placed on studies promoting physical exercise in the elderly, helping them to strengthen their functional physical condition (muscular strength, endurance, flexibility, balance) and risk of falls, allowing researchers to analyze the dangers and identify opportunities for improvement. The studies focus to increase the functionality of the elderly through the use of virtual games, FitForAll platforms, Cob, augmented reality, FLOW pillow.

A line of projects integrate innovative technologies to show content providing elderly people an opportunity to interact, share, enjoy aspects of everyday life. Use of digital television and its convergence between Telecommunications and IT should be promoted to support the development of interactive applications to optimize the management of medical knowledge linking the clinical and therapeutic fields to focus on prevention and diagnosis.

The present study serves as a starting point for the work that is currently being carried out on the use of interactive digital television to promote exercises that help to improve the gait of older adults.

References

Aal, K., Ogonowski, C., von Rekowski, T., Wieching, R., Wulf, V.: A fall preventive iTV solution for older adults. Siegen, Germany (2014). https://www.researchgate.net/profile/Kon stantin_Aal/publication/264503699_A_Fall_Preventive_iTV_Solution_for_Older_Adults/links/53e1ff330cf2235f352c003a.pdf

de Abreu, J.T.F., Almeida, P., da Silva, T.E.M.C.: Os telecuidados e a televisão interactiva. Envelhecimento, saúde e doença:novos desafios para a prestação de cuidados a idosos (2014). (in Portuguese). https://scholar.googleusercontent.com/scholar?q=cache:RTBz3gXbt6EJ:scholar.google.com/&hl=es&as_sdt=0,5. Accessed 15 June 2017

Agudo-Prado, S., Pascual-Sevillana, M.D., Fombona-Cadavieco, J.: Usos de las herramientas digitales entre las personas mayores. Comunicar: Revista Científica de Comunicación y Educación **20**(39), 193–201 (2012). (in Spanish). https://doi.org/10.3916/c39-2012-03-10

Al-khafajiy, M., et al.: Remote health monitoring of elderly through wearable sensors. Multimedia Tools Appl. (2019). https://doi.org/10.1007/s11042-018-7134-7

Anastasiou, A., Giokas, K., Koutsouris, D.: Monitoring of compliance on an individual treatment through mobile innovations. IFMBE Proc. **57**, 1237–1242 (2016). https://doi.org/10.1007/978-3-319-32703-7_238

Añaños, E.: La tecnología del «EyeTracker» en adultos mayores: cómo se atienden y procesan los contenidos integrados de televisión. Comunicar **22**(45), 75–83 (2015). In Spanish. https://www.redalyc.org/pdf/158/15839609008.pdf

Blanco, A.P.: Buenas prácticas del Proyecto Piloto Enred@ te: red social digital para personas mayores y voluntariado de la Cruz Roja Española. Cuadernos de Trabajo Social **29**(2), 201 (2016).

(in Spanish). https://www.fundaciontecsos.es/sites/default/files/noticias/51656-100034-2-pb. pdf

Castrillón, É.J., López Muriel, S.M., Prada Molina, M.S., Herrera, J.J., Cruz Amaya, M.M., Posso, D.Q.: Educación y participación a través de la itv: ¿está preparado nuestro medio? Revista Q 5(9), 1–25 (2010). (in Spanish)

Cisneros Perdomo, V., Carmona Ferrer, B., Cecilia, N.M.D., Chisholm, D.H., Sánchez Castillo, Y.: Eficacia de la plataforma Cobs en trastornos de equilibrio, postura y marcha del adulto mayor. Revista Cubana de Medicina Física y Rehabilitación 7(1), 42–54 (2015). (in Spanish). http://bvs.sld.cu/revistas/mfr/v7n1_15/mfr05115.htm

Dulva Hina, M., Ramdane-Cherif, A., Dourlens, S.: International Conference on Computer Systems and Technologies-CompSysTech'16 Serious Gaming: Autonomy and Better Health for the Elderly (2016). https://doi.org/10.1145/2983468.2983519

Epelde, G., et al.: Providing universally accessible interactive services through TV sets: implementation and validation with elderly users. Multimedia Tools Appl. 67(2), 497–528 (2013). https://doi.org/10.1007/s11042-011-0949-0

Giraldo-Rodriguez, L., Torres-Castro, S., Martínez-Ramírez, D., Gutierrez-Robledo, L.M., Pérez-Cuevas, R.: Tele-A y tele-alarma para adultos mayores: experiencias preliminares en México. Revista de Saúde Pública 47(4), 711–717 (2013). (in Spanish)

Godard, N., Pecci, I., Isokoski, P.: WeSlide: gestural text entry for elderly users of interactive television. In: Proceedings of the 11th European Conference on Interactive Tv and Video - EuroiTV '13, pp. 55–58 (2013). http://dl.acm.org/citation.cfm?id=2465963

Hamid, A., Foong, P.S.: Designing for patient-centred factors in medical adherence technology, pp. 40:1–40:4 (2012). http://dl.acm.org/citation.cfm?id=2501134.2501182%5Cn, http://dl.acm.org.libproxy1.nus.edu.sg/ft_gateway.cfm?id=2501182&type=pdf

Johnson, D.O., et al.: Socially assistive robots: a comprehensive approach to extending independent living. Int. J. Soc. Robot. 6(2), 195–211 (2014). https://doi.org/10.1007/s12369-013-0217-8

Kitchenham, B.: Procedures for performing systematic reviews. Keele University, Keele, UK, 3 February 2004, pp. 1–26 (2004). http://www.it.hiof.no/~haraldh/misc/2016-08-22-smat/Kitche nham-Systematic-Review-2004.pdf

Konstantinidis, E.I., Billis, A.S., Mouzakidis, C.A., Zilidou, V.I., Antoniou, P.E., Bamidis, P.D.: Design, implementation, and wide pilot deployment of FitForAll: an easy to use exergaming platform improving physical fitness and life quality of senior citizens. IEEE J. Biomed. Health Inform. 20(1), 189–200 (2016). https://doi.org/10.1109/jbhi.2014.2378814

Kyriazakos, S., et al.: eWALL: an Open-Source Cloud-based eHealth platform for creating home caring environments for older adults living with chronic diseases or frailty. Wireless Pers. Commun. 97(2), 1835–1875 (2017). https://doi.org/10.1007/s11277-017-4656-7

Lasheng, Y., Jie, L., Beiji, Z.: Research on a multi-agent based integrated health monitoring system for the elderly at home. In: Zhang, Y. (ed.) Future Wireless Networks and Information Systems, pp. 155–161. Springer, Heidelberg (2012)

Lo Bianco, M., Pedell, S., Renda, G.: A health industry perspective on augmented reality as a communication tool in elderly fall prevention, pp. 1–11 (2016). (in Spanish). https://doi.org/10.1145/2996267.2996268

Luna-García, H.: Patrones de diseño para mejorar la accesibilidad y uso de aplicaciones sociales para adultos mayores/Design patterns to enhance accessibility and use of social applications for older adults. Comunicar 23(45), 85–94 (2015). (in Spanish). https://search.proquest.com/docview/1707542527?accountid=38660

Martínez-Alcalá, C.I., Pliego-Pastrana, P., López-Noguerola, J.S., Rosales-Lagarde, A., Zaleta-Arias, M.E.: Adopción de las TIC en el Envejecimiento. In: Iberian Conference On Information Systems & Technologies/Conferência Ibérica De Sistemas E Tecnologias De Informação, CISTI Proceedings, pp. 1574–579 (2015). (in Spanish)

Matthies, D.J.C., Haescher, M., Nanayakkara, S., Bieber, G.: Step detection for rollator users with smartwatches, pp. 163–167 (2018). https://doi.org/10.1145/3267782.3267784

Miyoshi, H., Kimura, Y., Tamura, T., Sekine, M., Okabe, I., Hara, K.: Smart living - home rehabilitation training system using an interactive television. In: Lacković, I., Vasic, D. (eds.) 6th European Conference of the International Federation for Medical and Biological Engineering. IP, vol. 45, pp. 661–665. Springer, Cham (2015). https://doi.org/10.1007/978-3-319-11128-5_165

Molina, K.I., Ricci, N.A., de Moraes, S.A., Perracini, M.R.: Virtual reality using games for improving physical functioning in older adults: a systematic review. J. NeuroEng. Rehabil. 11(1), 156 (2014). https://doi.org/10.1186/1743-0003-11-156

Muntaner, A., Sampol, P.P., Conti, J.V.: Efectos de un programa de entrenamiento presencial vs prescripción a través de una aplicación móvil en personas mayores. Retos: nuevas tendencias en educación física, deporte y recreación 29, 32–37 (2016). (in Spanish). https://dialnet.unirioja. es/servlet/articulo?codigo=5400839

Nazário, D.C., de Andrade, A., Borges, L., Ramos, W.R., Todesco, J.L., Dantas, M.A.R.: An enhanced quality of context evaluating approach in the e-health sensor platform, pp. 1–7 (2015). https://doi.org/10.1145/2815317.2815320

Netto, A.V., Tateyama, A.G.P.: Avaliação de tecnologia de telemonitoramento e biotelemetria para o cuidado híbrido para o idoso com condição crônica. J. Health Inform. 10(4) (2018). (in Portuguese)

Ojetola, O., Gaura, E., Brusey, J.: Data set for fall events and daily activities from inertial sensors. In: Proceedings of the 6th ACM Conference on Multimedia Systems - MMSys '15, pp. 243–248 (2015). https://doi.org/10.1145/2713168.2713198

Organización Mundial de la Salud: Informe mundial sobre el envejecimiento y la salud (2015). (in Spanish)

Orso, V., Spagnolli, A., Gamberini, L., Ibañez, F., Fabregat, M.E.: Interactive multimedia content for older adults: the case of SeniorChannel. Multimedia Tools Appl. 76(4), 5171–5189 (2017). https://doi.org/10.1007/s11042-016-3553-5

Palacio, R.R., Acosta, C.O., Cortez, J., Morán, A.L.: Usability perception of different video game devices in elderly users. Univ. Access Inf. Soc. 16(1), 103–113 (2017). https://doi.org/10.1007/s10209-015-0435-y

Palipana, S., Rojas, D., Agrawal, P., Pesch, D.: FallDeFi. Proc. ACM Interact. Mob. Wearable Ubiquit. Technol. 1(4), 1–25 (2018). https://doi.org/10.1145/3161183

Park, R.C., Jung, H., Shin, D.K., Cho, Y.H., Lee, K.D.: Telemedicine health service using LTE-Advanced relay antenna. Pers. Ubiquit. Comput. 18(6), 1325–1335 (2014). https://doi.org/10.1007/s00779-013-0744-1

Parvin, P., Chessa, S., Manca, M., Paterno, F.: Detección de anomalías en tiempo real en el comportamiento de los ancianos con el apoyo de modelos de tareas. Proc. ACM Hum.-Comput. Interactuar. 2, EICS, artículo 15 (junio de 2018), 18 páginas (2018). (in Spanish). https://www21.ucsg.edu.ec:2117/10.1145/3229097

Urbauer, P., Frohner, M., David, V., Sauermann, S.: Rastreadores de actividad ponibles que apoyan a los ancianos que viven independientemente: un enfoque basado en estándares para la integración de datos en los sistemas de información de salud. In: En las Actas de la 8a Conferencia Internacional sobre Desarrollo de Software y Tecnologías para Mejorar la Accesibilidad y la Lucha contra la exclusión de la Información, DSAI 2018. ACM, Nueva York, NY, EE. UU., 302–309 (2018). (in Spanish) https://www21.ucsg.edu.ec:2117/10.1145/3218585.3218679

Picking, R., Robinet, A., McGinn, J., Grout, V., Casas, R., Blasco, R.: The Easyline+ project evaluation of a user interface developed to enhance independent living of elderly and disabled people. Univ. Access Inf. Soc. 11(2), 99–112 (2012). https://doi.org/10.1007/s10209-011-0246-8

Pùrez-Ugena y Coromina, Á., Salas Martínez, Á., Vizcaíno-Laorga, R.: Teleasistencia no invasiva mediante televisión digital: estudio de los hábitos de consumo de televisión de los mayores. Revista Latina De Comunicación Social **64**, 1–15 (2009). (in Spanish). https://doi.org/10.4185/rlcs-64-2009-850-632-645

Querol, V.A.: Las generaciones que llegaron tarde. Análisis de las prácticas sociales de los mayores en el ciberespacio. Editorial UOC, Barcelona (2011). (in Spanish)

Rao, A.K.: Wearable sensor technology to measure physical activity (PA) in the elderly. Curr. Geriatr. Rep. **8**(1), 55–66 (2019). https://doi.org/10.1007/s13670-019-0275-3

Ren, X., Visser, V., Lu, Y., Brankaert, R., Offermans, S., Nagtzaam, H.: FLOW pillow, pp. 706–713 (2016). https://doi.org/10.1145/2957265.2961841

Ribeiro, T., Santos, R., Moura, J., Martins, A.I., Caravau, H.: Application for older adults to ask for help from volunteers through television: design and evaluation of a high visual-fidelity prototype. In: Abásolo, M.J., Abreu, J., Almeida, P., Silva, T. (eds.) jAUTI 2017. CCIS, vol. 813, pp. 32–43. Springer, Cham (2018). https://doi.org/10.1007/978-3-319-90170-1_3

Sáenz-de-Urturi, Z., Santos, O.C.: User modelling in exergames for frail older adults, pp. 83–86 (2018). https://doi.org/10.1145/3213586.3226199

Santana, P.C., Anido, L.E.: Heuristic evaluation of an interactive television system to facilitate elders home care. IEEE Lat. Am. Trans. **14**(7), 3455–3460 (2016). http://www.ewh.ieee.org/reg/9/etrans/ieee/issues/vol14/vol14issue07July2016/14TLA7_57Santana.pdf

Santana-Mancilla, P., Anido-Rifón, L.: The technology acceptance of a TV platform for the elderly living alone or in public nursing homes. Int. J. Environ. Res. Public Health **14**(6), 617 (2017). https://www.mdpi.com/1660-4601/14/6/617

Saracchini, R.: Tecnología Al móvil, con realidad aumentada, para las personas mayores: a mobile augmented reality assistive technology for the elderly. Comunicar **23**(45), 65–74 (2015). (in Spanish). https://www21.ucsg.edu.ec:2080/docview/1707542640?accountid=38660

Scandurra, I., Sjölinder, M.: Diseño participativo con personas mayores: Diseño del futuro Servicios y refinamientos iterativos de servicios de eSalud interactivos para personas mayores Los ciudadanos. Med 2.0 **2**(2): e12 (2013). (in Spanish). https://doi.org/10.2196/med20.2729. eCollection 2013 Jul-dic. PubMed PMID: 25075235; PubMed Central PMCID: PMC4084776

Silva, T., de Abreu, J.F., Pacheco, O.R.: A utilização de um protótipo Wizard of Oz para a determinação de métodos de identificação automática de telespetadores seniores. Prisma.com **23**, 87–106 (2014). (in Portuguese). https://ria.ua.pt/bitstream/10773/15209/1/telmo_silva_final_Prisma.pdf

Spinsante, S., Gambi, E.: Remote health monitoring for elderly through interactive television. BioMed. Eng. OnLine **11**(1), 54 (2012). https://doi.org/10.1186/1475-925X-11-54

Stojmenova, E., Debevc, M., Zebec, L., Imperl, B.: Assisted living solutions for the elderly through interactive TV. Multimedia Tools Appl. **66**(1), 115–129 (2013). https://doi.org/10.1007/s11042-011-0972-1

Suyama, T.: A network-type brain machine interface to support activities of daily living. IEICE Trans. Commun. **E99B**(9), 1930–1937 (2016). https://doi.org/10.1587/transcom.2016SNI0002

Suyama, T.: Una interfaz de máquina cerebral de tipo red para apoyar las actividades de la vida diaria. In: En las Actas de la Conferencia conjunta internacional ACM 2017 sobre computación generalizada y ubicua y las Actas del Simposio internacional ACM 2017 sobre computadoras portátiles, UbiComp '17. ACM, Nueva York, NY, EE. UU., pp. 205–208 (2017). (in Spanish). https://www21.ucsg.edu.ec:2117/10.1145/3123024.3123142

Toribio-Guzmán, J.M., Parra Vidales, E., Viñas Rodríguez, M., Bueno Aguado, Y., Cid Bartolomé, M., Franco-Martín, M.A.: Rehabilitación cognitiva por ordenador en personas mayores: programa gradior. Aula **24**, 61–75, 216–218 (2018). (in Spanish). https://doi.org/10.14201/aula2018246175

Trujillo, J.C.G., Muñoz, J.E., Villada, J.F.: Exergames: una herramienta tecnológica para la actividad física. Revista Médica de Risaralda **19**(2) (2013). (in Spanish)

Tseng, K.C., Hsu, C.-L., Chuang, Y.-H.: Designing an intelligent health monitoring system and exploring user acceptance for the elderly. J. Med. Syst. **37**(6), 9967 (2013). https://doi.org/10. 1007/s10916-013-9967-y

Tsiachri Renta, P., Sotiriadis, S., Petrakis, E.G.M.: Healthcare sensor data management on the cloud, pp. 25–30 (2017). https://doi.org/10.1145/3110355.3110359

Vuorimaa, P., Harmo, P., Hämäläinen, M., Itälä, T., Miettinen, R.: Active Life home: a portal-based home care platform. In: Proceedings of the 5th International Conference on PErvasive Technologies Related to Assistive Environments - PETRA '12, pp. 1–8 (2012). https://doi.org/ 10.1145/2413097.2413133

User Experience

Individual Instead of User

Proposing a Better Word to Identify People Using Convergent Media Systems

Valdecir Becker[1]([✉]) [ID], Daniel Gambaro[2] [ID], Izaura D. Oliveira Magalhães[3] [ID], and Helder Bruno[1] [ID]

[1] Computer Science, Communication and Arts (PPGCCA), Informatics Centre, Federal University of Paraiba, João Pessoa, Brazil
valdecir@ci.ufpb.br, audiovisualdesign@lavid.ufpb.br
[2] Communications, Anhembi Morumbi University, São Paulo, Brazil
[3] Audiovisual Design Research Group, CNPq, João Pessoa, Brazil

Abstract. The purpose of this article is to discuss the different ways of using the term *user* and to suggest the replacement by the term *individual*. The word user is widely used in Computing, Library Science, and Mass Communication, meaning a person using a technology, or a digital system. However, the notion of use can be problematic in the context of media fruition, where the information received cannot be characterized just as simple use by user. In technological convergence, which unifies distinct areas such as interaction, production, and reception of content, people's relationship with technologies that mediate fruition becomes more complex than someone using a computer. To achieve the objective of this study, a narrative review was conducted in the scientific literature about the study of the term user and its evolution, uses and suggestions of new entries for the same purpose. The word that best describes a person using digital systems, interactive or otherwise, has been found to be *individual*. To exemplify the use of *individual* instead of *user*, three streaming services where analyzed.

Keywords: User · Individual · Computing · Media fruition · Evolution

1 Introduction

The use of the term *user* is common in different fields to define a person in front of a computer. However, with the advancement of modern technologies and forms of interaction and content enjoyment, questions were raised about the semantic scope of the entry. Authors in the field of Human Computer Interaction (HCI) consider that the word user is limited and does not fully express all aspects inherent to interactions with digital systems. In the Media Studies field, which include studies on audience and reception, other terms, such as audience, viewer, listener, cybernaut or reader, predominate to define the receiver, or consumer, of information. It is disregarded, for example, that the *reader* of a digital newspaper accesses it through the internet, also playing the role of cybernaut, or, more specifically, internet user. When watching a video inserted in a textual newspaper, the person assumes the role of *viewer* [1].

© Springer Nature Switzerland AG 2020
M. J. Abásolo et al. (Eds.): jAUTI 2019, CCIS 1202, pp. 159–172, 2020.
https://doi.org/10.1007/978-3-030-56574-9_10

Because of this semantic confusion, there is a tendency in the whole field of Communication and Information to generalize the term user when it refers to the use and fruition of digital content and systems. Thus, it is disregarded that the public of media products is composed of people with different repertoires, tastes and needs. This implies disregarding that audience's behavior is conditioned by contexts, both external and intrinsic, to each individual. Someone watching a TV program cannot be considered a user; In the same way, a person browsing a list of programs on a smart TV to choose which program to watch, is not a simple viewer, even if the program to be watched is the same.

This apparent disassociation of terms becomes more confusing when discussions related to software and interaction interfaces become part of the Communication universe, serving as a basis for production, distribution, access and fruition of information. The same connection can be applied to the HCI field, when it sets out to include concepts related to content during the software development. For example, multimedia and hypermedia systems are aimed at people who, possibly, will interact in different ways, with different meanings. Even as simple users of the system, different media interactions imply a multiplicity of uses, which the term user ends up limiting.

This article investigates this gap in terminology, the origins of the term *user* and its problematic application to explain the fruition of content in this totally interdisciplinary environment, which brings together previously distinct areas, such as HCI and Media Studies. As an outcome, it suggests the adoption of the term *individual*, which, from a sociological analysis, seems to better explain the current process of the relationship between people, technologies and content. To exemplify the limitations of the term *user* and the application of *individual*, fruition tests were carried out on three streaming services, which illustrates the complexity of the fruition process when audiovisual content and software are analyzed together.

2 Considerations About the Term *User*

To understand the mechanism used in application of the term user and its potentialities, or problems, we analyzed different areas using this word and how it is framed in Communication. According to the Portuguese language dictionary Priberam, a user is any person who uses the computer, programs, systems or computer services. [2] However, based on a narrative review of the literature, the term is also widely used to define a person who uses services of a library. Two of the most complete materials found during the research focus on studying this kind of user [3, 4].

The term user was initially disseminated in English and later translated into other languages. In all cases, the entry has as one of the first meanings the person who uses computer. Both systems based on command line, starting in the 1960s, and those based on graphical interfaces, such as Macintosh and Windows, in the 1980s, incorporated the term to designate different people using, shared and alternately, the same computer - thus guaranteeing a certain individuality of a technical nature (each user session carries the appropriate software) or of a personal nature (set of aesthetic and usability configurations). In all cases, a login is required to identify the person in front of the computer, which adapts the system according to existing profile and configuration.

Historically, the term user was disseminated in the 1940s. The first user studies were initiated at the Royal Society's Scientific Information Conference, in 1948, after the presentation of papers that instigated the concern with the user's needs [5].

In the field of media studies, the entry has become part of the terminology of the area when studies related to digital analog transition became common [1]. With the popularization of multimedia applications, loaded on personal computers with graphical interface and, later, on the WWW, the word became part of the common sense of the field, referring to anyone using a computer or interacting in digital networks, applications or websites (in this case, *user* started to be used as a complement or synonym for internet user, also named as cybernaut). In 2010 the INTERCOM Encyclopedia of Communication was published, which in the First Volume, Brazilian Dictionary of Communicational Knowledge - Concepts (terms, expressions and references essential to the study of the area) [6], presents 1097 entries, produced by 499 authors. The term user is mentioned throughout the document 78 times, to explain entries such as blogosphere, download, digital journalism, video game, among others. However, in addition to not being defined as a dictionary entry, no mention of the term user brings any definition.

2.1 Uses and Criticisms

In previous work, corresponding scientific works and literature were analyzed, finding gaps in information and surveys on the subject, especially within computing and communications fields [1]. Eleven texts were analyzed from searches performed using the keywords "user", "computer", "user in computing", "user history" and the respective Portuguese versions.

Even with the scope of the research, a small number of materials were found. However, when expanding the analysis to other areas, such as Information Systems, Librarianship and the pharmaceutical industry, it appears that it is a relatively well researched entry. The most complete studies on behavior, need and modes of use the entry user are focused on the area of Librarianship. Furthermore, despite the amount of current research, we have the problem that most of the materials that address the user's study in a comprehensive and historical way are quite old.

In the field of Communication, where software becomes part of the reception experience, studies on the adopted terminology are limited. The idea of a passive audience, common in classical communication theories, which receives messages and reacts in a limited way, even though producing and aggregating content, continues to prevail in the field analysis. Other authors have adopted the term user without questioning its scope and implications. "It is not surprising that it treats those who use technology only as users," says Alex Primo [7]), for whom the use of this word in computational spheres has been causing confusion, given the fact that the user presented in this way is merely a consumer. The introduction of the word *interactor*, proposed by Janet Murray [8] in the 1990s, frames something more to the role played by a person who experiences software, for example, as he or she will not necessarily only use what it offered, but also add, improve and employ new functions for certain products and/or systems [7].

[4] on the other hand, focusing on Librarianship, makes a counterpoint to the use of the term user, rethinking it in different fields of knowledge. Based on Alex Primo's research, quoted earlier, she suggests the term user connotes someone always at the mercy

of a superior being, thus promoting the presentation of the term *interact agent*, based on an idea of interaction. The author, then, presents an analysis of the entry interaction, in order to show how this word has been used, exposing that 50% of the total articles published on user study from 1970 to 2014 mention the term interaction (Table 1).

Table 1. Articles published on User Study (BRAPCI). Source: [4]

Period	Articles	Mentions of interaction
1970–1979	04	01
1980–1989	08	03
1990–1999	03	01
2000–2009	37	19
2010–2014	28	15
Total	80	39

It is notorious the greater use of the word according to the years. This is due to greater attention given to the subject, in addition to emergence of some areas, such as HCI, which after its dissemination in several areas, promoted, from the 1980s, the user experience concept, especially in the fields of computing and software development.

2.2 Limitations to Determine Interactivity

The discussions related to interactivity brought the term user to the Communications field, especially regarded to Media Studies. Along with interactivity, the software also became part of the analysis, as it is responsible for the interaction, both in simply computational systems, as in digital television or in mobile applications [9]. In the radio area, the first studies to mention a *user listener* are from the 1990s, referring to "Usina do Som" and software for computers based on website services [10]. The concept brought by interactivity proposes a new configuration in the communication process, with actions between two parties, which will result in participation of the interlocutors and intervention of all those involved [4].

Interactivity, therefore, provides the possibility of exchanging information, for example, between software and those who are *on the other side of the screen* (or the speaker). The information is passed on to this *user* through an addition of data and an interaction made between the human and the computer. In a help chat, for example, of those existing on several shopping sites, one person does more than simply use a system, he or she also generates data to receive information. Another analysis can be made by expanding the reasoning to Digital TV or video systems on demand, where the *viewer* uses the remote control, or a keyboard, to search for information interacting with software. When entering personal data, the following recommendations and search results are affected, generating feedback from the system. Thus, there is an interaction that goes far beyond simple use.

As we will demonstrate below, the limitation of the user concept becomes evident when the result of the interaction is not an action to be performed by software, or an answer expected by a person. If the result of the interaction is a media product to be consumed in the system itself, several substitutions of the person's status may occur during the act of fruition.

The advancement of user studies provides a new perspective on who we are working with, giving us a clearer and broader interpretation of who these people are, what their needs are and what pleases them. This fact is due, as already mentioned, to HCI, which has been proving the importance and the advantages of thinking and adapting products and systems to the human being needs, demands and desires. Proposals, such as Human-Centered Design, expand the user's vision for an experience that encompasses, in addition to effectiveness and efficiency, satisfaction and improves human well-being, accessibility and sustainability [11].

3   The Sociological Definition of *Individual*

The word *individual* is so common in studies on society, it has such a clear meaning, that we rarely pay attention to the semantic load it carries. It is, above all, a term that initially makes it possible to build the duality between the human and the set in which he finds himself: the individual is a constituent part of a collectivity or society. It should be noted, beforehand, that a *project of the individual* was built mainly from the enlightenment theories: as "subject of reason, the individual was valued for his potential knowledge and his ability to transform the world" [12]. It is at this moment that the idea of the individual as *being indivisible* is strengthened, with freedom of choice and subject to his own history. Therefore, as far as we are concerned in this article, the term individual brings, at its root, the idea of interaction with the environment and the ability to connect in a network, safeguarding a certain unity.

Of course, as Social Studies has shown since [13], there are certain "coercive powers" acting externally on individuals and shaping people's actions in balance with society itself. A Marxist base would claim that these powers are structures, or social institutions like State, family and market, that guide behavior, customs, economics; in short, culture. It is important to note that this is not the only possible view to explain people's behavior in life and in society, especially in the urban and industrial context consolidated between the 19th and 20th centuries. However, it is not possible, within the scope of this article, to make a rereading of social theories and discussing how each one observes the action of social forces on individual actions, limiting the supposed freedom of individuals' choice[1].

It remains, here, to understand how the individual is perceived within some areas of Social Studies, which will lead us to understand how individualism (or individualization) becomes a contemporary value that, we argue, ends up being replicated in all forms of cultural production - even in a complex audiovisual system.

Usually the term individual served to define his position (or opposition) in relation to the collectivity, especially when it constitutes a *crowd* or *mass*. The expansion

---

[1] For a detailed review of the theories, see [32].

of urban centers since the middle of the 19th century, especially due to the increasing industrialization and constitution of cities, the establishment of nation-states and modern bureaucracies, demanded from social scientists more complex explanations to describe behavior of large groups of people. If, until this new configuration of urban spaces, traditions and religions provided enough material to maintain a certain cohesion, industrial society breaks with these ties. Jesus Matín-Barbero [14], in his most famous book, provides a broad explanation of how the first theorists regard the "masses" as indistinct, suggested and passive in the face of the world, since they are hampered by specific culture and tradition. Only in the 1930s, as the author notes, psychoanalysis and American functionalism begin to indicate that "mass culture" respects and incorporates the notions of individuality, especially by trying to understand how people deal with anonymity in through the crowd. Although the notion of *mass* prevails in the study of the media, especially on radio at first, and then on TV, it becomes insufficient to explain the dynamics that lead people to act in a similar way, even when distinct spaces. According to sociologist Renato Ortiz, "the anonymity of big cities and corporate capitalism pulverizes existing social relationships, leaving individuals 'lost' in the social mesh" [15].

The social *experience*, or the way in which individuals act in society and interact with their empirical realities, is an important addition to understand how culture is affected by the mass media. The definitions of Culture given by Raymond Williams [16] become important here: a global social order, built in daily life and readjusted according to the performance of the collectivity, which organizes society and the practice of individuals. It is noted, therefore, that the individual and society can only be considered together, since the essence of one is the result of the existence and action of the other [17].

Individuals need to find *meanings* in what they do and consume, that is, they need to experience a certain product, art or practice as part of their unique lives, to then share them with the collective [16]. The complexity of modern and industrialized societies, determined by the advance of capitalism and market economies - such as the cultural market -, adds new forms of symbolic interaction with reality. The consumption of physical and symbolic products becomes a relevant experience in the formation of individual's identities. Issues such as representativeness and identification are incorporated into technological design, opening doors to different forms of product appropriation, as well as the construction of strategies of belonging or distinction in social groups [18]. Ortiz states that "society must therefore invent new instances for the integration of people… one of these instances is advertising" [15].

This evolution of society as a result of consumption starts to indicate social changes that were determined by the political and economic organization of the world after the Second World War. There is a dispersion of social agendas, at the same time, industries focused on cultural production diversify and start to serve different *niches*. Simultaneously, marginal sectors of society gain relevance, mainly economically and culturally. Examples can be found especially in the 1960s, such as sexual freedom movements, student demonstrations and the intensification of the racial debate that marked changes in various parts of the globe [19]. According to Hall, this is a trait of postmodernity: identity becomes a "mobile celebration".

At that moment, the formation of an imaginary around individual autonomy stands out. The same sense of "freedom of choice" for the rational individual, pointed out even in the 19th century, is reconstructed within the social, cultural and market logic that dominates contemporary times. Thus, marketing campaigns start to elaborate the person as a unique, cohesive individual [15, 19], and stand out from the crowd that is part.

This notion of individualization based on identities of multiple references is, in part, result of the reorganization promoted by economic and cultural globalization [19]. The universal becomes a value of the contemporary era, in which barriers would not be welcome - at least, from the point of view of monetary circulation, commodities and information [20]. Notions like "global village" become dominant in media discourses. As a counterpart, cultural fragmentation and the multiple possibilities that individuals have to build and show themselves in front of others, emphasized by economic logics in the 20th century, become elements of distinction, either of social position or of cultural formation [21].

The offer of products - physical or symbolic - is based on diversity, so that people's strategy is to accentuate their individuation, through the choice of products they use, the brands they display, and consumed cultural products (films, music, series for TV, comics). This is not a complete difference: there is a certain standardization of the products offered, but without becoming a general rule that makes everything exactly the same. These small differences allow some industries to move from a high volume logic, that is, to sell a lot and constantly, to a high value logic, in which the highest production cost, due to the attempt to create an impression of customization, is amortized by the higher value of the product [15]. The higher cost is justified, on the consumer side, by the symbolic values acquired from consumption, as widely theorized by Cultural Studies [18].

The height of the intensification of the search for individuality, we can say, started in the 1990s. With the multiplication of communication tools, information is also fragmented, atomized, and becomes another component within this set of pieces that the individual uses to compose his identity. The social experience itself, increasingly based on media devices [22], is also fragmented.

The popularization of the web adds tools accentuate the feeling - and the need - of fragmentation and individualization [23]. Two parallel processes occur here, especially due to the use that people apply to digital tools for sharing content. First, the individual idealizes an identity with which he works in a network, which can be more or less faithful to what he really is in other spheres [24]. This expression of a relatively coherent self is, in essence, the construction of a personal networked narrative whose object is representation and visibility before the other, to communicate something about oneself [25]. The second process is the way in which software interprets a set of data made available by individuals when using digital tools. There is a set of relationships made possible by software's reading of person's profile, to retain them as a user of a certain system, and answers must be consistent with the profile that subject projects of himself (while also representing the interests of the firm using the data collected).

We can conclude, then, that the process of *assembling* an identity, today, involves the appropriation of multiple fragmented economic and cultural references, in correspondence with the ephemerality with which daily life is experienced. The ease of connection emphasizes transience, which allows the individual to feel a sense of belonging to several social groups at the same time, even for a short duration. Stuart Hall [19] refers to this phenomenon using the term subject instead of individual, because indivisibility (at least, from a sociological point of view) is questioned: "The subject assumes different identities in different moments, identities that are not unified around a coherent 'me'. Within us there are contradictory identities, pushing in different directions, in such a way that our identifications are being continually displaced".

We then entered the 21st century with this imaginary. This article is not about praising or criticizing the emphasis on the individual and the continuous reconstruction of identities. What we intend with this brief exhibition is to highlight that these are the social values present in social experience, with which audiovisual producers must deal. The result that is presented, therefore, is an infinity of interactions people can undertake between themselves, and between them and the world, in search of the composition of an identity that is, at the same time, unique and shared. Likewise, people need to deal with the increased sense of anonymity, a consequence of multiple connections via social media. It should also be noted that there is a sense of autonomy in the choices made by individuals, even if driven by marketing tools, and this feeling is, in most cases, much more fundamental than the unique identity and built from totally free choices.

3.1 Mediatized Experience

Considering all the historical burden the word individual carries, we understand that it provides important subsidies to identify the person who uses a complex audiovisual system. [17], when revisiting different theories about a sociology focused on the subject, as opposed to the idea of the individual, points out that "the individual is a complex, bio-psycho-social set. It cannot be reduced to one or the other of its dimensions. He is a human being in the flesh, who has a character, a physique, an identity, a social status, a marital status, a family history, ways of being, speaking and doing; as well as, someone who has explicit or implicit projects, beliefs, desires and fantasies"(p. 68).

The adequacy of the term *individual* also depends on another phenomenon widely discussed in the field of Communications: the expansion of the sphere of media in everyday life. It is a theme addressed in different biases, all referring to what we can call, generically, "mediatization theories".

There is a common trait to different authors who approach mediatization: it refers to the expanded use of technological instruments and devices to perform daily tasks, including communication. These effects have been studied for some time. [26] signaled a change in the interactional processes (among people, with institutions and with the environment), so that mediatized interactions would become the reference process - which, effectively, materialized: the forms of interaction and contact are, today, especially selected from a perspective that takes into account the permanent connection, and the *analog* forms are seen as exceptions or in the process of transformation. According to [27], mediation indicates that culture and society become increasingly dependent on media, so that a *media logic* starts to shape communication and interaction. In this way, the set of media now has, among its functions, enabling a domain of shared human experience.

According to [28], mediatization explains the complexification of society due to a progressive incorporation and predominance of communication technologies, a phenomenon occurred in different waves since the invention of the written press. We are experiencing a profound mediatization, in which our surroundings operate under limitations, affordances and power relations that emanate from media. Also, according to the authors, the socialization and interaction infrastructures created in the last two decades (especially databases and algorithms), affect the construction of everyday reality. Thus, practices within the different spheres of life are intertwined and conditioned to technical devices, which is enhanced by the total digitalization and mobility of communication devices. The sense of device, then, must be reviewed in the light of the human experience affected by these aspects of mediatization.

We can consider that, in general, technical objects tend to become technical devices, as they become concrete and acquire their technical individuality, throughout the sociogenetic process, and are thus integrated into the human experience of the world. When reaching a high level of incorporation in the human organism, technical devices do not only constitute the experience, but become part of the experience that human beings have in the world [29].

In other words, the mediation devices[2] delimit a *reality effect*, that is, the conditioning of reality to the devices' form. Even before this phase of profound mediatization, [22] demonstrated the capacity of media enunciation devices to anticipate, model and replace the real, creating an "effect of the real". [29], however, remember that human experience does not depend on technical objects - these, in turn, are human creations according to outstanding real-life needs. The experience is linked, mainly, to the options made individually or collectively by people. According to the authors, it is an illusion media devices replace human behavior and activities, and this is due to the high degree of performance achieved by technological development.

We can conclude, then, that even if people are overloaded with the media ecosystem and the excess of stimuli, they are still social beings with individualized behavior, even if impacted by the dominant logic of media. However, the opposite seems more plausible to us: since all technological development is a response to cultural and social demands, in a continuous path of incorporation into the experience itself, maintaining the sense of identity and individuality in the relationship between people and technology seems to correspond more directly to the contemporary moment[3].

4   Analysis: The Case of Streaming Services

In order to discuss the semantic relationship of meanings between user and individual, the interaction and the content proposal of the three main streaming services available in Brazil: Netflix, Amazon Prime and Globoplay, were analyzed. It is noticed that, from the perspective of the content offer, subscribers are treated as users, in the sense of simple use of the platforms. There is some level of customization but limited primarily by restrictions imposed by software programming. The graphical interfaces seek to promote

---

[2] It is important to note that Rodrigues and Braga refer, as mediation devices, to everything that mediates reality. In the case of communication devices, they give the name "mediation devices", a subcategory, therefore.

[3] Such reinforcement, we understand, does not negate the sense of belonging and social representation. However, it is necessary to expand investigations to demonstrate the effectiveness of these individualized processes, within global media sets, for the strengthening of groups.

a fluid interaction between the software and the audiovisual content, which makes the user experience pleasant, but limited in terms of identification.

The tests were carried out at the Laboratory of Interaction and Media (LIM), at the Federal University of Paraíba (UFPB). Scripts with task descriptions divided into stages to be achieved were applied to five participants. Two types of scripts were designed: one for films and other for series. These scripts consisted of a sequence of activities, where the volunteer performed interface navigation tasks such as: navigating the system's main page; looking for a film at the request of the mediator in the way he deemed most appropriate; doing the same search using the search engine; changing subtitles before and during the fruition; looking for extra content about what was being displayed. The test was recorded on video, allowing researchers to subsequently access all information given by the participants, since the actions taken by them were simultaneously commented on (think aloud).

The objective was to detect difficulties or usability errors in the interface. One difficulty found by the participants, for example, was that they were unable to change the audio or subtitles of the content on Amazon's Prime Video during the fruition. Post-test questionnaires were also carried out, not with the aim of generating any relevant social data - impossible due to the number of participants in the research - but with the aim of generating a complement and a better interpretation and support the analysis of the obtained data.

The data analysis in the study revealed that intuitive and fluid navigation in the system is extremely important for the user. Elements of interaction design have the greatest impact on this experience, providing a full understanding about what is available in each interface. At this point, Netflix was considered a better experience than Prime Video. However, if we consider only this experience, users should prefer the Globo Play service, instead of Amazon's Prime Video, since that platform has also shown an intuitive design and fluid interface for navigation. But this was not the case. The point is that Prime Video offers universal and exclusive content (own productions, as Netflix), with excellent design and complete descriptions. We can notice the interaction (navigation between screens, routes and different levels, the response time and the fluidity) and the offer of extra contents, which complement the user experience, have complementary importance (Table 2).

Analyzing the research from the fruition point of view, another problem is perceived: the limitation represented by the recommendation algorithms, often inappropriate to the profile of each individual. We understand that this is mainly the result of the *user* treatment given to service subscribers. This results in less adequacy of the interface and offers at an individualized level. Even common actions that lead to a certain inertia or passivity, such as simply watching a soap opera chapter, already represent a diversity of roles played by individuals. This is not covered by the way products are distributed in these services.

Imagine a situation of complete fruition: an individual, when turning on the TV to watch a certain channel, can be classified as viewer. However, from the moment he opens an Electronic Program Guide on Digital TV to read a film synopsis, or when he decides to open the Netflix application, installed on SmarTV, to watch episodes from a TV show, he starts to use a pre-installed computer system. In addition, when the continuation of

Table 2. Summary of the study outcomes

System	Netflix	Prime Video	Globo Play
System fluidity	Fluid	Restrained	Fluid
Extra content	Reduced	Excellent	Reduced
Search tools	Fast response (real time); good redundancy in viewing content information	Slow response (latency); confused interface	Fast response (real time); no redundancy of content information
Interface navigation	Satisfactory; well-organized interface elements	Confused; unpredictable; poorly organized interface elements.	Good; well-organized interface elements

fruition depends on that person's action, he is constantly mixing the roles of viewer and user. At this point, it is important to highlight that the choice of the workpiece to be watched, and the willingness to interact with the system, are fueled by identification processes: personal tastes and inclinations tend to be important factors in this dynamic, and the term user does not include either.

The scenario becomes more complex when we imagine that, soon, these platforms will start to offer complex audiovisual workpieces, which imply greater action by the people who are watching. The test carried out by Netflix, with the film "Black Mirror: Bandersnatch", exemplifies the limitations and raises a series of questions. First, restrictions on the platform itself seem to have led to limitations of the script alternatives; second, this demonstrates that there is still no technology available that allows a total customization of the workpiece; or a more elaborate action of sharing and co-participation in production. HBO's West World series is a good example of fans' appropriation of material available from the series universe. Since the first season, discussion sites, fanfics and several theories have been moving the spectators' performance. However, the dispersed way in which this occurs denotes the division of roles that people play on each platform: on TV, they must be passive and attentive viewers; on the HBO app, users can afford to binge watch the series; and on social media and websites, people build their identities in true participatory economies, as described by [30].

Thus, more than users, we are talking about appropriation by individuals who use the narrative to develop identities within these groups of fans. Systems that will support works with such complexity must also offer less customization restrictions and more co-participation options. Considering the fact that access to communicational media has promoted its incorporation into everyday experience, then it is necessary to effectively overcome the semantic barriers of user definition. At first, even the terms *interact agent* and *interactor* seem more conducive and can be used in certain situations to define the role occupied by individuals. These, however, do not understand the alternation of people's roles during the extended act of fruition. Interact agent or interactor tend to overestimate the moments of action, with interaction through hardware and software interfaces, to the detriment of a processes represented by choices and moments of passive fruition, without interaction. The objective of watching a film or series is multifaceted: moments of relaxation and entertainment, defined by the bias of liking, which result is a pleasant experience.

User, interact agent and interactor, used in isolation, are terms that are unable to classify or explain this physical, emotional and psychological experience that can be provided by the incorporation of audiovisual activity in the experience. If we consider multimedia systems, this gap in the term is aggravated, given that individual choices must also be understood as instances of strengthening identities based on cultural consumption.

5   Conclusion

This article discussed the use and application of the term user and suggests replacing it with the term individual. The word user is widely used in computing, librarianship and communication, meaning a person who uses a technology or a digital system. However, this notion of use becomes problematic in the context of media fruition, where the exchange of information between the human being and the computer system cannot be characterized by the simplistic relationship of use by a user. In technological convergence, which unifies different areas such as creation, interaction, production and reception of content, the relationship of people with technologies that mediate fruition becomes more complex than this description done by *use*. From a narrative review in the scientific literature, it was realized that the criticisms of the entry are varied and consistent.

Thus, the present article suggests that the word individual best describes a person who uses digital systems, mediatized or not. The term individual presents itself as a viable solution to understand the role each person assumes in audiovisual consumption designed within the logic of interactivity. Among the points that contribute to this, we find vast references of Cultural Studies in discussing the processes of identity. The identification that people process in contact with consumable products - whether physical or not - are part of a process of individualizing consumption. In the case of radio and television, for example, Raymond Williams already identified, in the 1970s, the deepening of a "mobile privatization" given by the fruition contexts of these productions [31].

Even though it is important to discuss how the process of individualization of consumption impacts social organization and its mobilization. The role cultural appropriations of goods, given in a relatively independent and individual way, has in the construction of the self is relevant. Matching the audiovisual production to the wishes of a person, who wants to appropriate aspects in the construction of a *lifestyle*, means giving elements both for the construction of an individual image, as well as belonging to a larger group. It is, in the end, the correspondence to an important modern value: individuality composed of an eclectic presence. Its exploration opens up fields to even discuss the renewal of the socio-cultural importance of a product (we immediately think of soap operas and series, historically a field of debate on everyday themes).

Considering audience is multiple, composed of a very large diversity of individuals with their own characteristics, the audiovisual producer also starts to access a very wide set of possible values for his product. The overlapping of possible and similar uses, in this sense, becomes part of the workpiece planning process, its structure, capable of meeting requirements that go beyond the immediate and uncompromised fruition.

From a more technical point of view, cultural relations with technology - or, more precisely, with interfaces - can also translate into more appropriate responses to personalization. What is sought, therefore, is an elastic process sufficient to adequately encompass different levels of individuals' skills, far from the standardization that the user assumes. Perhaps more lasting relationships can be created with interfaces, which are configured in a new layer of meanings inserted in the message.

Finally, the term individual exposes the contradictions that may exist between the producer's expectations and the multiple expectations of individuals, as varied as each personality. The manifestations of these contradictions can, in the organization of the system, gain space to be evident and, transformed into data, more easily guide the organization of actions without the fixation of a single: the recognition of multiplicity, allied to the already mentioned personalization, can guide the creation of an adaptive system of audiovisual consumption, individual and based on the load of human cultural experience.

References

1. Magalhães, I., Becker, V.: O Termo Usuário: Histórico, Significados e Aplicabilidade para a Comunicação. Trabalho apresentado no 42º Congresso Brasileiro de Ciências da Comunicação (2019). http://portalintercom.org.br/anais/nacional2019/in-dex.htm
2. "Usuário" (2008–2020). In Dicionário Priberam da Língua Portuguesa. http://www.priberam.pt/dlpo/chave
3. Siatri, R.: The evolution of user studies. Libri **49**(3), 132–141 (1999)
4. Corrêa, E.C.: Usuário, não! Interagente: proposta de um novo termo para um novo tempo. Encontros Bibli: revista eletrônica de biblioteconomia e ciência da informação **19**(41), 23–40 (2014)
5. Vickery, B.: The royal society scientific information conference of 1948. J. Doc. **54**(3), 281–283 (1998)
6. Sociedade Brasileira de Estudos Interdisciplinares da Comunicação. Enciclopédia INTERCOM de Comunicação, São Paulo (2010)
7. Primo, A.: Enfoques e desfoques no estudo da interação mediada por computador. Intercom, San Francisco (2003)
8. Murray, J.: Hamlet no Holodeck. Unesp, São Paulo (2003)
9. Becker, V.: A evolução da interatividade na televisão: da TV analógica à era dos aplicativos. Lumina, vol. 7, no. 2 (2013)
10. del Bianco, N.R., Moreira, S.V., (eds.) Rádio no Brasil: Tendências e Perspectivas, pp. 185–204. EdUERJ, Rio de Janeiro. UnB Brasília
11. ABNT: NBR ISSO 9241-210: Ergonomia da interação humano-sistema Parte 210: Projeto centrado no ser humano para sistemas interativos. Rio de Janeiro (2010)
12. Barreira, I.A.F.: O lugar do indivíduo na sociologia: sob o prisma da liberdade e dos constrangimentos sociais. Revista das Ciências Sociais **34**(2), 51–63 (2003). http://www.periodicos.ufc.br/revcienso/article/view/33924
13. Durkheim, É.: O que é um fato social? In: Botelho, A., (org.) Essencial Sociologia [Versão Kindle]. Penguin Classics Cia das Letras, São Paulo (2013)
14. Martín-Barbero, J.: Dos Meios às Mediações: comunicação, cultura e hegemonia (2ª edn.). Editora UFRJ, Rio de Janeiro (2003)
15. Ortiz, R.: Cultura brasileira e identidade nacional, 5ª edn. Brasiliense, São Paulo (1994)

16. Williams, R.: Cultura: Sociología de la comunicación y del arte. Barcelona. Argentina: Ediciones Paidós, Buenos Aires (1982)
17. Gaulejac, V.: O âmago da discussão: da sociologia do indivíduo à sociologia do sujeito. Cronos 5(1/2), 59–77 (2005). https://periodicos.ufrn.br/cronos/article/view/3233
18. du Gay, P., Hall, S., Janes, L., Madson, A.K., Mackay, H., Negus, K.: Doing Cultural Studies: The Story of Sony Walkman (2ª edn.) Sage Publications, Londres. The Open University, Milton Keynes (2013)
19. Hall, S.: A identidade cultural na pós-modernidade, 7ª edn. DP&A Editora, Rio de Janeiro (2003)
20. Ortiz, R.: Universalismo e diversidade. Boitempo, São Paulo (2015)
21. Gambaro, D.: Bourdieu, Baudrillard e Bauman: O consumo como estratégia de distinção. Novos Olhares 1(1), 19–26 (2012). https://doi.org/10.11606/issn.2238-7714.no.2012.51444
22. Rodrigues, A.D.: Experiência, modernidade e campo dos media (1999). http://www.bocc.ubi.pt/pag/rodrigues-adriano-expcampmedia.pdf
23. Bauman, Z.: Vida para consumo: a transformação das pessoas em mercadorias. Jorge Zahar Editor, Rio de Janeiro (2008)
24. Bruno, F.: Monitoramento, classificação e controle nos dispositivos de vigilância digital. Revista Famecos 15(36), 10–16 (2008). https://doi.org/10.15448/1980-3729.2008.36.4410
25. Thompson, J.B.: A nova visibilidade. Matrizes 1(2), 15–38 (2008). https://doi.org/10.11606/issn.1982-8160.v1i2p15-38
26. Braga, J.L.: Mediatização como processo interacional de referência. Animus – Revista Interamericana de Comunicação Midiática V(2), 9–35 (2006). https://periodicos.ufsm.br/animus/issue/view/407
27. Hjarvard, S.: The mediatization of culture and society [Versão Kindle]. Routledge, Londres (2013)
28. Couldry, N., Hepp, A.: The Mediated Construction of Reality: Society, Culture, Mediatization. Polity Press. (versão ePub), Cambridge, Malden (2017)
29. Rodrigues, A.D., Braga, A.A.: A Natureza Midiática da Experiência. In: Barreto, E., Barreto, V.S., Paiva, C.C., Moura, S., Soares, T., (eds.) Mídia, Tecnologia e Linguagem Jornalística, pp. 188–202. Editora do CCTA, João Pessoa (2014)
30. Jenkins, H.: Cultura da convergência. Aleph, São Paulo (2008)
31. Williams, R.: Television: Technology and Cultural Form. Schocken Books, Nova York (1975)
32. Giddens, A.: Sociologia, 4ª edn. ArtMed Editora, Porto Alegre (2005)

Author Index

Printed in the United States
By Bookmasters